Gary Ashwill writes the baseball history blog "Agate Type: Adventures in Baseball Archeology" (agateype.typepad.com). He has won the John Coates Next Generation Award from the Jerry Malloy Negro League Conference, and compiles the SABR Baseball Research Award-winning Seamheads Negro Leagues Database (www.seamheads/NegroLgs.index.php).

Sol White's Official Base Ball Guide

BY
SOL WHITE

Introduction and Notes
by Gary Ashwill

© 2014 by Summer Game Books
Introduction and notes copyright © 2014
by Gary Ashwill

All Rights Reserved.

No part of this publication may be reproduced, stored in a retrieval system, or transmitted in any form or by any means—electronic, mechanical, photocopying, recording, or otherwise—without the written permission of the publisher.

978-1-938545-21-4 (print)
978-1-938545-22-1 (eBook)

For information regarding permissions, bulk purchases, or additional distribution, write to Summer Game Books, PO Box 818, South Orange, NJ 07079-0818, or info@summergamebooks.com
www.summergamebooks.com

CONTENTS

Introduction by Gary Ashwill ix

Sol White's Official Base Ball Guide 1
    Sol White 5
    Colored Baseball 9
    Championship Contests 40
    Notable Feats of Colored Pitchers 63
    Colored Base Ball as a Profession 75
    Managers' Troubles 81
    The Color Line 87
    Old Timers Compared 105
    The Cubans 109
    How to Pitch, by Andrew Foster 113
    Art and Science of Hitting,
        by Grant (Home Run) Johnson 119
    Casey at the Bat 123
    When Casey Slugged the Ball 129
    Colored Players and the League 140

Notes by Gary Ashwill 143
    Who's Who in the Sol White Guide

PUBLISHER'S NOTE

Summer Game Books is pleased to be publishing this new edition of *Sol White's Official Base Ball Guide*. We have aspired to match the original edition as closely as possible in terms of the exact wording of the text, the cropping of the photographs, and their position in the book.

This edition also features a wealth of background information on both author "King Solomon" White, and the ballplayers White played with, managed, and competed against in the early years of organized black base ball.

Sol White was a star player and influential leader from the 1890's through the formation and launch of the Negro National League in 1920. But by having the vision to make a detailed record of the greatest players, teams, and feats from this fascinating yet largely unknown chapter of baseball history, his contributions to the game may have a greater impact today than they did 100 years ago.

INTRODUCTION
By Gary Ashwill

In the spring of 1907 a team called the Philadelphia Giants started selling a small paperbound book at their games. Its cover said it was the *History of Colored Base Ball*, by Sol White, captain of the Giants, the "World's Colored Champions." Inside, the title page named it *Sol White's Official Base Ball Guide*, and added that it had been edited by H. Walter Schlichter (who also held the copyright). At 5 ¾ by 3 ½ inches, it could be described as a thick pamphlet or even a "brochure," as White would later call it.[1] The book's 128 pages were packed with tiny print and photographs illustrating the exploits of professional African American ball clubs and their players going back a little more than 20 years. It also featured essays on "How to Pitch," by Rube Foster, the best black pitcher in the country, and "The Art and Science of Hitting," by Grant Johnson, the best black everyday player. Like a game program, it was sprinkled with advertisements, mostly for businesses related to the Philadelphia Giants or run by the owners of other black teams, as well as a few other Philadelphia-area concerns. And for good measure it reprinted "Casey at the Bat" and one of its sequels, "When Casey Slugged the Ball."

Just four years earlier, W. E. B. DuBois had declared in *The Souls of Black Folk* that "the problem of the twentieth century is the problem of the color-line." It was certainly baseball's problem. The tentative reconstruction era that baseball had undergone in the 1880s, when dozens of black players, and a few black teams, infiltrated the minor leagues and even (briefly) the majors, had shuddered to a halt in the 1890s. The last black player to appear in organized baseball was Bill Galloway, who played in five games for the Woodstock club of the Canadian League in 1899. By 1907 a "veil," as DuBois would put it, had descended over the world of black baseball. Sol White's little book was a guide to this world.[2]

Even as the minor leagues were struggling with the idea of racially-integrated dressing rooms, all-black professional teams were forging ahead, finding opponents and venues, attracting crowds, making (at least some) money. Sol White identified the Cuban Giants, founded in 1885, as the first black professional club; in fact, they were "neither giants nor Cubans," and may not have been the first professionals.[3] But they did make by far the biggest splash on the sporting scene of any African American team to that point, getting dates with big league clubs within only a few weeks of their founding. They spawned imitators and competitors, and so many of them called themselves "Giants" that the name eventually became a code word or euphemism meaning "black baseball team." By the time Sol White was leading the Philadelphia Giants, dozens of African American professional or semiprofessional clubs (most of them Giants of one sort or another) dotted the country.

But this was not yet the era of the Negro leagues. The teams were not organized, and did not actually spend most of their time playing each other. In 1903, for example, the Philadelphia Giants played 130 games, but only 7 of those were against other black professionals. The rest were against white teams—minor leaguers, college teams, semipros. It's crucial to understand that the world Sol White describes in his *Guide* was a sports world very different from anything we'd recognize now. The minor leagues were free and existed for their own sake, to run their own pennant races, rather than just to develop players for the majors. And beyond the minor leagues were the independent professionals, or semipros. They represented small cities and towns that weren't in leagues—but they also existed in big cities like Chicago, New York, and Boston. In those pre-television, pre-radio days there was a huge demand for live baseball, and even Philadelphia, with two major league teams, had room for a more local, and cheaper, brand of diamond entertainment.

A reporter, writing about Sol White in 1927, said that he had "given his life, unselfishly, to the game purely for the love of it… Some others went into the game to make money, and made it, but Sol takes greater pride in having watched the game develop to where it is today, although he has no money to show for it."[4] No doubt this is true; still, as this book shows, money was greatly important to White, both as a player and as a manager. He was, after all, trying to make a living, and later trying to keep money-making enterprises afloat. It's worth reflecting that in 1907 slavery was still well within living memory, and that it was even more recent in the 1880s when White begins his story. Several of the original Cuban Giants—and most of Sol White's immediate family—were born in slave states before the Civil War. Though their early histories are not known in detail, it seems virtually certain that some of them were born into slavery—or at the very least possessed intimate knowledge of the institution. Now they were attempting to make baseball their profession. And while this was a possible path for African American men around the turn of the century, it was not an easy one, and it did not typically produce a stable, steady career progression—as a look at Sol White's own life and career shows.

Sol White the Ballplayer

Sol White's family background is hazy, though there are a few things we do know. He was born (as he tells us) in Bellaire, Ohio, just across the Ohio River from Wheeling, West Virginia, on June 12, 1868. His parents and four older siblings were all born in Virginia; the circumstances of the family's arrival in Ohio remains unknown. Within two years of his birth his father was dead and his mother, Judith White, a washer woman according to the 1870 census, was raising five children alone.[5] As a boy Sol hung around a local team called the Globes. One day in 1883, playing against a Marietta, Ohio, team captained by Ban Johnson (who would go on to found the American League), a Globes player hurt his finger and had to come out of the game—so they drafted Sol to take his place.[6]

He had heard stories of Bud Fowler, the black professional ballplayer.[7] The Cuban Giants had been founded in 1885, and Frank Grant joined the Eastern League and then the International League in 1886. Consequently the idea of a career in baseball for a black man may not have seemed so far-fetched to Sol. When the

National Colored League started up in 1887, he saw his chance, and earned a spot on the Pittsburgh Keystones. Unfortunately the league didn't live up to Sol's ambitions. It crashed within a couple of weeks, leaving players stranded hundreds of miles from home with no money, and while the Keystones struggled through as an independent team, Sol went back home to sign with the Wheeling club of the Ohio State League.

It's clear that had he been white, he would have been a huge major league prospect. As a 19-year-old third baseman with Wheeling in 1887, he batted .370 and slugged .502, with 20 extra base hits in 53 games. His teammate, the catcher/outfielder Jake Stenzel, hit .387 and slugged .474, with 8 extra bases in 41 games. Stenzel would go on to play over 700 games as a major league outfielder, batting .338 with a 134 OPS+. Eventual Hall of Famer Ed Delahanty, the same age as White, hit .351 and slugged .475 as a second baseman for the Mansfield club in the same league—and wound up hitting .346 in the big leagues, with a 152 OPS+. While Delahanty and Stenzel were certainly outliers (there were other comparable hitters in that league who did not go on to great major league careers), the fact remains that White as a player was showing similar abilities at a similar age, and would certainly have gotten every chance to make a similar mark in the majors if it weren't for the color line.[8]

What happened next was Sol White's first substantial experience with baseball Jim Crow. In the off-season the league (now renamed the Tri-State League) passed a rule barring all black players. The *Wheeling Register* noted that "[v]ery many of our citizens will regret this on account of Sol. White, as he was a favorite with the patrons of the game in this city, being not only one of Wheeling's best players, but also a perfect gentleman in his actions."[9] Weldy Walker, the former major leaguer and catcher for the Ohio State League's Akron team, wrote a fiery letter denouncing the action, which was published in *The Sporting Life*.[10] Within a few weeks the ban was rescinded. The president of the Wheeling club, aware of White's popularity, promptly signed him and sent him to meet the team at Lima, Ohio—but the new manager, Al Buckenberger (who would later manage the Pittsburgh Pirates), apparently did not want a black player on the team, and White was turned away.[11]

With the exception of one interlude in 1895, White would spend the rest of his career on all-black teams, although a few of them would play in white leagues. For the rest of the 1888 season he re-signed with the Pittsburgh Keystones. In August he accompanied them to a four-team "Colored Championship" tournament put on by John M. Bright in New York. The Keystones finished second to Bright's own Cuban Giants.[12]

The next few years were a whirlwind of teams and leagues for White. Although primarily an infielder, he played virtually every position. Like all the other best black players of this era, he was caught up in the battle between the Cuban Giants and their arch-rivals, the New York Gorhams, who competed both on the field and off, constantly raiding each other for players. White spent two different spells with the Gorhams, and all or part of five seasons with the Cuban Giants. He also played for the

1890 York Colored Monarchs, a white-owned club that signed up most of the 1889 Cuban Giants; a revived version of the Pittsburgh Keystones in 1892; the Boston Monarchs in 1893; the Hotel Champlain team in Bluff Point, New York, which was organized by the head waiter Frank P. Thompson, one of the men who had founded the Cuban Giants; the Fort Wayne, Indiana, club in the 1895 Western Interstate League (White's last experience in a white minor league); and the Page Fence Giants of Adrian, Michigan, one of the great black teams of the nineteenth century. At various times his teams played in the Middle States League, the Eastern (and Western) Interstate League, the New York Semiprofessional League, and the Connecticut State League. During these years his wages advanced from the paltry $10 a week he earned as a catcher/infielder with the '89 Gorhams to the $75 to $80 a week he got from the '95 Page Fence Giants and Ft. Wayne teams.[13]

Two key developments in White's life took place after he spent the 1896 season with the Cuban Giants. First, he entered Wilberforce University as a preparatory student, and spent the next four years playing ball in the summer and studying in the winter. Second, he left the Cuban Giants for the Cuban X-Giants. The "X" signified "ex-Giants," as the team had been founded when a group of Cuban Giants became fed up with John M. Bright's sharp dealing and left. They engaged Edward B. Lamar to be their business manager, and played on the "cooperative plan," "a system whereby all expenses were deducted from the gross receipts and the balance evenly distributed between the players."[14] White had stayed loyal to Bright for one season after the X-Giants revolution, but eventually decided to join. Put together, his entrance into college and his defection to the co-op team seem to indicate an interest in bettering his situation, achieving a measure of self-determination.

His next stop, after leaving school, was the Columbia Giants of Chicago. They were formed in 1899 when the Columbia Club, an organization of young black businessmen in Chicago, purchased the Page Fence Giants from their white backers.[15] After another season with the Cuban X-Giants, White teamed up with H. Walter Schlichter, sports editor of the *Philadelphia Item* (a white paper), and Harry Smith, baseball editor of the *Philadelphia Tribune* (a black paper), to found the Philadelphia Giants. For the first time Sol White would serve as captain and manager.

"The Strongest Organization of the Time"

Now he entered the years that he would later consider "the heyday of his glory," the years when he made the Philadelphia Giants champions and wrote the book that might be his true legacy. The Philadelphia Giants kicked up a rivalry with White's old team, the Cuban X-Giants, that echoed the Gorhams/Cuban Giants rivalry of the previous decade, especially in the propensity of the two teams for raiding each other's players. In 1903 the Cuban X-Giants, behind a young fireballer from Texas named Andrew Foster, defeated White's Giants 5 games to 2 to claim the "colored base ball championship of the world."[16] So

White and Schlichter signed Foster from the X-Giants, along with Charlie Grant and a young Pete Hill. When they met the X-Giants again for the black championship a year later, Foster set the tone by striking out 18 of his former teammates in the first game, and Philly took the series 2 games to 1.[17]

In 1905 White brought in the X-Giants captain and manager, Grant Johnson (who had actually twice been White's manager, with the Page Fence Giants and Columbia Giants), along with their lefthanded ace, Danny McClellan, and the coup was complete. Now he had what he called "the strongest organization of the time."[18] The Giants won 134 games, lost only 21, and tied 3, sweeping four games against the Newark International League team and winning nine out of ten games (tying the tenth) against the Brooklyn Royal Giants, the only major black team they faced that year.[19]

They could not stay on top for long. The 1905 Philadelphia Giants, for all their impressive firepower, were a precarious financial balancing act; they were too dominant, and had trouble booking enough truly high-profile games against worthy opponents. E. B. Lamar of the X-Giants, having been robbed of nearly all his stars, refused to meet the Giants; so did the All-Cubans, the team of Cuban League stars run by Abel Linares. So in 1906, when those erstwhile punching bags the Royal Giants offered Grant Johnson a big salary to be their player-manager, White and Schlichter couldn't stop them. Soon after, a new club called the Quaker Giants, run by the McMahon brothers from New York, signed away Bill Monroe and Chappie Johnson.[20]

Despite these setbacks, the Giants won the 1906 championship of the local, racially-integrated International League of Independent Professional Base Ball Clubs, as well as the informal colored championship. That same year Sol White wrote his *Official Base Ball Guide*, outlining the history that had led up to this point. Unfortunately, just as he had already lost Grant Johnson to the Royal Giants, he now lost Rube Foster (and a couple of other players) to the Leland Giants of Chicago. White compensated by bringing in a young second baseman named John Henry Lloyd from the Cuban X-Giants (which disbanded after 1906) and making him into a shortstop. The International League was replaced by the avowedly black National Association of Colored Professional Base Ball Clubs, organized by Schlichter and New York promoter Nat C. Strong. The Giants won their second straight pennant, which doubled as their fourth straight blackball championship.[21]

Difficulties continued to beset the club in 1908, including more defections—Rube Foster signed away Pete Hill and Emmett Bowman (who was one of White's particular favorites)—and the death of pitcher George Washington ("the Georgia Rabbit"), who suffered a heart attack in the team's dressing room before a game he was scheduled to pitch in Winsted, Connecticut.[22] White and the Giants persisted. They even ventured into the lion's den in Chicago and managed to tie Foster's Lelands, 3 games to 3.[23] But in the end they lost the black championship of the National Association to Grant Johnson's Royal Giants. More damagingly, the partnership at the heart of the team, between White and Schlichter, broke up. In later years White admitted to being "high strung" during this period, which may have contributed to their falling out. Whatever started the "misunderstanding," it led to White leaving the team and joining the Quaker Giants for 1909—whereupon Schlichter had White and his club, along with another black team, Pop Watkins's Stars, "outlawed" by the National Association. Observers noted that this amounted to "the white managers of the colored clubs" keeping out the black managers.[24]

"The Peer of All Managers"

In 1910 Sol White was hired to manage the Royal Giants, but only after Schlichter agreed to remove him from the National Association's blacklist.[25] According to the sportswriter Harry Daniels, two of the Royal Giants' best players, outfielder/pitcher Charles Babcock Earle and shortstop Bill Monroe, ignored White and seemed to be the "real bosses themselves." Daniels criticized John W. Connor, the Royal Giants' owner, for hiring the "peer of all managers" and then not allowing him to do his job.[26] One might wonder if White was losing his touch. If so, it didn't stop the McMahon brothers from appointing him in 1911 to organize their new team, the Lincoln Giants, which was to play in Harlem's Olympic Field. White signed John Henry Lloyd and outfielder Spottswood Poles. When in July he plucked the "crack battery" of youngsters Dick Redding and Louis Santop from the roster of the Philadelphia Giants, he sealed the fate of his old team—Schlichter disbanded the Giants within weeks.[27]

At the same time White had assembled the core of the next great African American baseball team, one that in 1913 would defeat Rube Foster's American Giants for the "negro baseball championship of the United States." Sol White would not be around to savor this victory, however. Before the Lincolns' first season was even over, he had left the team for unspecified reasons, replaced as manager by Lloyd.[28]

White made one last stab at success in fast company. For the first time he left the U.S. in pursuit of his baseball career, joining the Fe club in the Cuban League, and staffing it with black American players. It was a collaboration with his old ace pitcher, Rube Foster—both brought players from their respective 1911 teams, plus a few more from the St. Louis Giants and Leland's Chicago Giants. Unfortunately, the cream of African American baseball at the time—Joe Williams, John Henry Lloyd, Pete Hill, and Grant Johnson—had all joined the Habana club. The Sol White-Rube Foster team-up got off to a slow start, and the Fe management was exceedingly impatient. They lost five of their first six games, culminating in a 13 to 2 humiliation by Habana on January 29, 1912.[29] After this game seven of the American players plus White were let go.[30]

That was the end of the primary phase of Sol White's career at the top of the African American baseball world. In 1912 he was reported to be organizing a team owned by Ambrose Hussey, a well-known white promoter, to play at the Ridgewood Grounds in Brooklyn.[31] Apparently it was called the "Boston Giants," even though it was organized in New York. This team made no stir whatsoever—there was virtually nothing about it in the press, and White (through Calvin) later admitted that "business was dull" that year.³² Despite rumors that White and Schlichter had gotten together again to revive the Philadelphia Giants, or that White would undertake to manage the Pittsburgh Giants, in fact he retired from the game. He went home to Bellaire, Ohio, for the first sustained period since he began playing ball in 1887.³³

Whatever he did in Bellaire during his retirement, around 1918 White began to get restless, evincing a renewed interest in baseball, and talking about putting together a team in Columbus, Ohio.³⁴ In 1919 he wrote a series of articles for the *Cleveland Advocate* on black baseball. Meanwhile his old ace pitcher, Rube Foster, had founded the Negro National League (NNL). After its first season, the Dayton Marcos franchise was moved to Columbus and renamed the Buckeyes, and White joined the organization as secretary. Lloyd was engaged as player-manager for the 1921 season, but despite his and White's efforts, the team sank to sixth place place and folded at the end of the season.

He reemerged right away in 1922 as manager of a second-tier club in Cleveland, the Fears Giants, and followed this up by taking to the dugout as field manager of another NNL team, the Cleveland Browns, in 1924 (his first manager's job at the highest level in a dozen years).³⁵ White brought in his old third baseman from the Philadelphia Giants, the 45-year-old Bill Francis, and one of his outfielders was the 19-year-old Vic Harris, who would become a legendary manager for the Homestead Grays in the 1930s. But in the end the Browns were no better than the

Buckeyes. Under White's tutelage they went 11-20. He left in early July, replaced by the team's catcher, Otto "Jaybird" Ray.[36]

Shortly afterward he seems to have moved east. In December 1924 he disclosed a plan to W. Rollo Wilson of the *Pittsburgh Courier* to create a farm team for the Eastern Colored League (ECL) that would take players on loan from the various league clubs and "bring them up to major league ability."[37] While it's unclear whether this plan ever saw fruition, in 1926 he became involved with a new ECL club, the Newark Stars. The "young and progressive manager," Andy Harris, signed White as coach and advisor.[38] Wilson commented that "in his day" White "was cock o' the walk and the king-pin strategist of Negro baseball. Now he comes back to the game he knows and loves so well, and the week's salute goes to him, the mighty somnambulist of a vanished dream (if Mons. V. Hugo will pardon me)."[39] But all White's experience and Harris's youth and new ideas didn't avail the Stars, who won only one of the eleven ECL games they managed to play before they folded up.[40] This was the last big league team he was ever involved with.

"A Wealth of Information"

Sol White may have retired from baseball, but that didn't mean he had lost interest in the sport. In 1927 a major article by Floyd J. Calvin about his life and career, evidently based on extensive conversations with White, appeared in the *Pittsburgh Courier*. White "has been close to the game since its beginnings in 1885," Calvin wrote, "and he hardly talks about anything else."

He certainly wrote about it extensively. A second printing of *Sol White's Official Base Ball Guide*, presumably for sale during the 1908 season, added 9 more pages of text entitled "History of Colored Base-Ball During 1907." It's possible that the original intention was to produce subsequent editions, updated annually with such supplements. This wasn't to be. But reportedly by 1927 White had a second volume already written, described by Calvin as "a kind of second edition to his old one, bringing the game from 1907 down to date, and if there is anybody anywhere in sports circles who thinks enough of what has gone before to help Sol print his record, he will be glad to hear from them."[41]

Over the next decade White produced a series of columns and stand-alone articles for eastern African American newspapers, mostly the *New York Age* and *New York Amsterdam News*. It could be that some of these pieces were drawn from the manuscript mentioned by Calvin. In a 1936 letter, Schlichter suggested that White go "see the Editor of your colored paper and try to sell him a history of colored baseball which you could write either as a single article or as a series. Except for recent years you have all the data in the book and I would be glad to furnish the cuts and pictures. It looks to me to be worth trying."[42] He was evidently unaware that White had already been writing such articles for years. As late as 1940 White was still consulting Schlichter about "the feasibility of another brochure with a more elaborate discussion, or rather, comments about teams, managers and players, the 'game' and the pertinence of the business…"[43]

Meanwhile the reputation of his little 1907 book grew, even as actual extant copies of it dwindled. By 1927, Calvin was writing that "Sol's personal copy of his own book is the only one he knows about and it would be a historical tragedy if this should be lost."[44] In 1936 H. Walter Schlichter had two copies left. He agreed to send one to White, who had evidently requested it, but "[t]he other one I will not part with at any price."[45] In 1953 a collector of baseball guides placed an appeal in the *Pittsburgh Courier*, hoping that copies of White's book "may be in the hands of your subscribers who are no longer interested in them."[46] The sportswriter Malcolm Poindexter, Jr., penned a column about White's book in 1954. "Few copies are available today," he wrote, "but in the text is a wealth of information about the beginning of professional baseball....What a pity such great heritage is lost in the pages of a few volumes."[47]

Despite its lack of availability (until recent decades) *Sol White's Official Base Ball Guide* has exerted a tremendous influence on our understanding of the early black game. Its value was already clear when it was first published. Promotional copy that ran in both the *Indianapolis Freeman* and the *Baltimore Afro-American* was pretty accurate:

> "Sol White's 'History of Colored Base Ball' is just off the press. It is unique, in that no history of the popular pastime, as played by colored men, has ever before been written. No one knows more of the progress of the game better than he, and he writes most entertainingly. In addition to the full tale of the progress of the game there are nearly a hundred

half-tone pictures of old-time and present-time colored players, including all of the present-day celebrities, and a number of groups of the prominent teams of this and past years."[48]

The ad copy rightly concentrated on the book's visual content, which is considerable (if overstated; the book actually contained 57 images rather than "nearly a hundred"). While some of the photographs here circulated independently of White's book, most of them are known only from these pages. The formal studio photographs of the Cuban Giants players in suits and ties are particularly valuable, historically speaking; for many of them, these are the only known images other than an appearance or two in team photos.

The book carried a significance beyond the photographs, of course. It has helped shape our perceptions of early black baseball, especially in its focus on the Cuban Giants as the first African American professional team. While it's hard to establish particulars in all cases, professionalism of one sort or another certainly antedated the Cubans. Philadelphia, for example, was said in 1882 to possess a "nine of colored professionals," most likely the Orions, one of the Cuban Giants' predecessors. The 1883 St. Louis Black Stockings were called "colored professionals," as were the 1883 Gordon Club of Chicago and the (black) 1884 Metropolitan Base Ball Club of New York.[49] As was the case with white baseball, it seems probable that professionalism grew in stages, and that there was no hard clear line dividing the amateur from the professional era. In general, Sol White exhibits a (pardonable) bias toward events in the northeast, with a few nods to Chicago. There's no mention of the 1886 Southern League of Colored Base Ballists, which preceded the National Colored League by one year as the first Negro league.[50]

Another notable characteristic of White's *Guide* is its complete lack of statistics. It's without a doubt the most striking difference between this *Official Base Ball Guide* and the Reach and Spalding guides, which were *mainly* statistical compendia. The vast majority of Giants games were not league games, of course, and even the International League of 1906 and the National Association of 1907-1909, with very limited schedules of championship games, never published any individual playing statistics. One guesses that, as captain, manager, and sometime player, White simply didn't have time to compile statistical summaries from score sheets, and didn't have the money to hire someone to do it for him. The best he could do was to reprint box scores that were more or less identical to the box scores that appeared in the *Philadelphia Item* and other daily papers. Due to lack of resources and (to some extent) lack of interest on the part of team owners, problems with statistics would afflict African American baseball as long as the color line held, eliciting many complaints from fans, journalists, and players themselves.

It might be an exaggeration to claim that before *Sol White's Official Base Ball Guide*, there was no such thing as black sportswriting—but it would not be too much of one. Even in the black press, published material about African American baseball teams and players was largely confined to box scores, game accounts, and brief items. After White published his book, everything began to change. Black baseball journalism became an identifiable genre. The *Indianapolis Freeman* led the way, opening its pages to the likes of Dave Wyatt, Cary B. Lewis, James H. Smith, and Harry Daniels, who wrote analyses and prognostications, picked all-star teams, and argued with each other. The *New York Age*, *Chicago Defender*, and *Indianapolis Ledger* followed suit, pointing toward the golden age of black sportswriting in the 1920s, when nationally-distributed papers like the *Defender* and the *Pittsburgh Courier* devoted two or three whole pages to sports each week.

If Sol White's book was unique in its day, it remained unique for decades afterwards. There were a few pamphlets published about black baseball, along with programs, some short-lived magazines, and yearbooks, and of course there was the voluminous newspaper coverage over the years. But there were no *books* solely devoted to the Negro leagues and African American diamond exploits—nothing with the scope and ambition of White's history, nothing that brought all the threads together and gave them shape and meaning the way he did. There were experts and scribes (Dave Wyatt, W. Rollo Wilson, Frank Young, Halley Harding, and many more) who could have produced a whole library of books, on baseball and other sports, if they'd been given the chance. But it wasn't until the 1970s that Sol White's magnum opus would at last find companions to sit beside it on the bookshelf of black baseball history.

Sol White would live to see Jackie Robinson finally break the color line in 1947. He would live to see Larry Doby and Roy Campanella and Don Newcombe follow Robinson. He would live to see the arrival of Minnie Miñoso and Willie Mays, before he finally passed away in 1955. While we have no record of his thoughts about these momentous events, we should count ourselves fortunate that history did preserve his detailed accounts of baseball behind the color line from a half-century before.

DURHAM, NORTH CAROLINA
FEBRUARY, 2014

Notes

1 Letter: Sol White to H. Walter Schlichter, 15 January 1940. See Frank Ceresi and Carol McMains, "Sol White's 'History of Colored Base Ball'," The National Pastime Museum. http://www.thenationalpastimemuseum.com/article/sol-whites-1907-history-colored-base-ball Accessed February 28, 2014.

2 W. E. B. DuBois, *The Souls of Black Folk* (1903; New York: Library of America, 1986), 3.

3 "Notes and Comments," *The Sporting Life*, September 5, 1888, 2. On professionalism see note 46 below.

4 Floyd J. Calvin, "Sol White Recalls," *Pittsburgh Courier*, March 12, 1927, Second Section, 4

5 1870 and 1880 United States Census.

6 Johnson actually attended Marietta College—it's unclear whether he was captaining the school's baseball team or, as one 1927 article about Sol put it, "a hick town club" (Calvin, op. cit.).

7 Calvin, op. cit.; "Sol White Recalls," *New York Age*, December 27, 1930, 6.

8 Statistics from Baseball-Reference.com.

9 "Base Ball—Some Midwinter Gossip Concerning the Sport," *Wheeling Register*, December 1, 1887, 4.

10 "Why Discriminate? An Appeal to the Tri-State League By a Colored Player," *The Sporting Life*, March 14, 1888, 5.

11 "Bellaire," *Wheeling Register*, May 27, 1888, 3.

12 "For the Colored Championship," *New York Sun*, August 27, 1888, 3.

13 Calvin, op. cit. On the York Colored Monarchs see Michael E. Lomax, *Black Baseball Entrepreneurs, 1860-1901: Operating By Any Means Necessary* (Syracuse: Syracuse University Press, 2003), 108-112; on the revived Pittsburgh Keystones, see "Morris-Madden," *Cleveland Gazette*, April 16, 1892, 1; on the New York Semiprofessional League and the Connecticut State League, both of 1891, see Lomax, op. cit., 116-117.

14 Calvin, op. cit. Like much of Calvin's article, this is most likely Sol White's explanation of the co-op system, which Calvin either transcribed or paraphrased.

15 "The Columbia Club's Colored Champions," *Illinois Record*, March 18, 1899, 3.

16 "Cuban X-Giants Win First Game," *Philadelphia Inquirer*, September 13, 1903, 14;

17 "Phila. Giants Trim Cuban X-Giants, Foster Fanning 18 Men at Plate," *Philadelphia Inquirer*, September 2, 1904, 6; "Phila. Giants Win Championship," *Philadelphia Inquirer*, September 4, 1904, 12.

18 Calvin, op. cit.

19 On the 1905 Philadelphia Giants, see Phil S. Dixon, *American Baseball Chronicles: The 1905 Philadelphia Giants* (Charleston, S.C.: BookSurge, 2006).

20 Calvin, op. cit.

21 "A New Local League," *The Sporting Life*, April 14, 1907, 17.

22 "Ball Player Drops Dead," *Washington Post*, July 2, 1908, 8.

23 Sol White, "Sol White Recalls," *New York Age*, January 10, 1931, 6.

24 Lester A. Walton, "Baseball Notes," *New York Age*, April 15, 1909, 6; Lester A. Walton, "Baseball Notes," *New York Age*, April 22, 1909, 6.

25 Walton, "Sol. White to Manage Royal Giants," *New York Age*, May 5, 1910, 6.

26 Harry Daniels, "Season of 1910 in the East," *Indianapolis Freeman*, January 7, 1911, 7.

27 Lester A. Walton, "Philadelphia Giants Disband," *New York Age*, August 3, 1911, 6.

28 "Lloyd Succeeds White as Manager," *New York Age*, September 14, 1911, 6.

29 "El Juego de Ayer," *El Mundo*, January 30, 1912, 9.

30 "Wholesale Release of Players in Cuba," *New York Age*, February 15, 1912, 6.

31 "Making Ready for Baseball in the East," *Indianapolis Freeman*, March 16, 1912, 7.

32 Calvin, op. cit.

33 "Poles Quits Lincolns and Joins Royals," *New York Age*, June 13, 1912, 6; "Will Have One of the Strongest Colored Teams," *Indianapolis Freeman*, April 26, 1913, 7; Calvin, op. cit.

34 "Sol White to Have Fast Baseball Nine," *Chicago Defender*, February 2, 1918, 10.

35 Allen H. Dorsey, "White Lead Fears," *Cleveland Gazette*, June 24, 1922, 2; "Browns Open Next Sunday," *Cleveland Gazette*, April 12, 1924, 1.

36 "The Browns Win Both," *Cleveland Gazette*, July 19, 1924, 2.

37 W. Rollo Wilson, "Eastern Snapshots," *Pittsburgh Courier*, December 27, 1924, 12.

38 J. M. Howe, "Sport Sidelights," *Philadelphia Tribune*, April 17, 1926, 11.

39 W. Rollo Wilson, "Eastern Snapshots," *Pittsburgh Courier*, April 17, 1926, 14. Hugo's "might somnambulist" was Napoleon.

40 "Newark Stars Quit Eastern League, Players Disbanded," *Pittsburgh Courier*, July 10, 1926, 14.

41 Calvin, op. cit.

42 Letter, H. Walter Schlichter to Sol White, 18 July 1936. Jerry Malloy, compiler, *Sol White's History of Colored Base Ball, with Other Documents on the Early Black Game 1886-1936* (Lincoln: University of Nebraska Press, 1995), 157.

43 Ceresi and McMains, op. cit.

44 Calvin, op. cit.

45 Letter, Schlichter to White, op. cit.

46 William Puckner, "Collector of Baseball Guides Makes Appeal," *Pittsburgh Courier*, February 21, 1953, 11.

47 Malcolm Poindexter, Jr., "Sports I View," *Philadelphia Tribune*, May 3, 1954, 11.

48 Untitled item, *Indianapolis Freeman*, May 18, 1907, 7; "History of Base Ball," *Baltimore Afro-American*, May 11, 1907, 4.

49 "Notes," *Cincinnati Enquirer*, July 22, 1882, 5; "Red and Black," *The Inter Ocean* (Chicago), June 19, 1883, 5; "Local Gossip," *New York Globe*, March 8, 1884, 3. See also Lomax, op. cit., 49.

50 "A Colored Base Ball League," *Charleston News and Courier*, April 8, 1886, 8.

Sol. White's

OFFICIAL

Base Ball Guide

BY

SOL WHITE

Captain

Philadelphia Giants

Champions

1905-1906-1907

Edited by

H. WALTER SCHLICHTER
Philadelphia, Pa.

COPYRIGHT, 1907
BY
H. WALTER SCHLICHTER

Preface

Since the advent of the colored man in base ball, this is the first book ever published wherein the pages have been given exclusively to the doings of the players and base ball teams.

Realizing the great progress made, and the interest displayed by the players and the public in general, I have endeavored to follow the mutations of colored base ball, as accurately as possible, from the organization of the first colored professional team in 1885, to the present time, in the trust that it will meet the approbation of all who may peruse the contents of this book.

To the players and managers of the past and present and the patrons of colored base ball, to them I dedicate this book.

SOL WHITE

SOL WHITE
Captain and First Baseman
Philadelphia Giants

Sol White

Sol White was born in Bellaire, O. June 12, 1868, and learned to play ball when quite a youngster. When but 16 years of age he attracted the attention of managers of independent teams throughout the Ohio Valley and his services were in great demand. His original position was short stop, but by playing on different teams, he developed into a great all-round player filling any position from catcher to right field.

His first professional engagement was with the Keystones, of Pittsburgh, a member of the Colored League, in 1887. He was assigned to left field and later was placed at second base, where he played brilliantly.

After the Colored League disbanded he was signed by Wheeling, W. Va., of the Ohio League, and assigned to third base. He stood second in batting among the members of his club with an average of .381. In 1888 the color line was drawn in the Ohio League and he played with independent teams during the season.

In 1889 he signed with the Gorhams, of New York, as a catcher, but was assigned to second base where he finished the season.

During 1890 he was a member of the famous York Monarchs, the team that won the pennant in the Pennsylvania League.

In 1891 he joined the "Big Gorhams" composed of former players of the York team.

From 1892 to 1895 he was with the genuine Cuban Giants. 1895 found him with Fort Wayne, Ind., in the Western Inter-State

League. The league disbanded in June and he finished the season with the Page Fence Giants, of Adrian, Mich.

After the season of 1895 closed, Sol began a course at Wilberforce University. From 1896 to 1900 he played with the C. X. Giants in the Summer and attended school during the Winter. In 1900 he left school and joined the Columbia Giants of Chicago. In 1901 he played second base and captained the Cuban X-Giants. In 1902 he organized the Philadelphia Giants and has been captain ever since. Under his guidance the Philadelphia Giants have won the championship of the world every year since.

No colored ball player has had a wider experience in base ball than Sol, and no ball player has profited by experience greater than he has.

Colored base ball owes a great deal of its popularity of late to his hard, earnest, indefatigable work.

Washington's Manufactory

314 North Broad Street,
PHILADELPHIA, PA.

Be l 'Phone

Washington's Custom Made Shirts, and Waiters' Supplies.

Also a full line of Ladies' and Children's Wearing Apparel; large stock of Sidecombs, Ruching-pins, Collars, Handkerchiefs, etc.

High-grade Stationery, Finest Perfumes, and all kinds of Toilet Articles.

An unexcelled supply of the best and most delicious Confectionery.

S. K. GOVERN
Manager of the Original
Cuban Giants

Colored Baseball

Babylon, L.I., has the distinction of being the birth-place of the first professional Colored Base Ball team in the world.

It was at Babylon in 1885 that Frank P. Thompson, head-waiter of the Argyle Hotel, chose the best ball players from among his waiters, and organized a base ball club to play as an attraction for the guests of the hotel. He appointed Ben Holmes, third base and Capt.; A. Randolph, first base; Ben Boyd, second base; Wm. Eggleston, short stop; Guy Day, catcher; Geo. Parego, Frank Harris and R. Mortin, pitchers; Milton Dabney, left field and Chas. Nichols, right field.

They played nine games at Babylon against the strongest teams of New York city and Long Island, winning six, losing two and tieing one.

The calibre of ball displayed by the men, led Thompson to start them on the road as professionals. After the hotel season closed, which was about the middle of September, they left Babylon for Philadelphia.

At this time, there was a team of colored ball players in Philadelphia known as the "Orions" which had been beating every independent team in the vicinity of Philadelphia. The boys from Babylon met them, and took them into camp by a score of 6 to 4.

At this time, the Babylon boys were under the management of John F. Lang (white) of Philadelphia. Mgr. Lang signed at once, three of the best players on the "Orion" team, viz. Geo. Williams, second base and Capt.; Abe Harrison, short stop; and Shep Trusty, pitcher. This move on the part of Lang was one of the most important and valuable acts in the history of colored base ball. It made the boys from Babylon the strongest independent team in the East and the novelty of a team of colored players with that distinction made them a valuable asset, which was taken advantage of by Mr. Walter Cook, of Trenton, N. J.

After defeating the "Orions" they met and defeated Philadelphia's crack white team. This team was composed of such well-known players as, Mike Drennan, Gordon Simpson, Boleau Brill, Montgomery Zinn, Collins and Kelly. The colored boys beat them 10–8.

After several games of small importance, they got a chance to demonstrate to the world that they were not out as a novelty alone. They proved their ability and gained great respect as a baseball team by defeating the Bridgeport, Connecticut, team, champions of the Eastern League, by a score of 5–4. This was the game which by their winning, gave them an advantage which has never been enjoyed by a colored team since their entrance into base ball. Walter Cook a capitalist of Trenton, N. J., became their backer; S. K. Govern (colored) their manager, one of the finest base ball grounds in the country their home and "Cuban Giants" their name.

When Mr. Cook signed his men for the following season of 1886, they were the happiest set of men in the world. As one of them told the writer, not one would have changed his position with the President of the United States.

At that time salaries were according to positions. Mr. Cook gave pitchers and catchers, $18.00 per week and expenses; infielders, $15.00 per week and expenses; outfielders $12.00 per week and expenses.

Eighteen hundred and eighty-six saw the Cuban Giants with a line-up picked from all over the country. With the exception of F. Grant, Walker and Fowler, they had the best the colored base ball world could produce. With Clarence Williams and Arthur Thomas as catchers; Billy Whyte, Shep Trusty and Geo. Stovey pitchers, they were as strong in battery work as any team in the country. Jack Frye, first base, Geo. Williams, second base, and captain, Ben Holmes, third base, and Abe Harrison, shortstop, composed an infield that was fast, tricky and heady. Boyd, in centre field as a regular, and Billy Whyte in left (very fine fielder in those days), and a catcher in right, composed the outfield. The strongest line-up of the Giants this year would have been; C. Williams, catcher; Stovey or Trusty, pitcher; J. Frye, first base; G. Williams, second base; Holmes, third base; Harrison, shortstop; Whyte, left field; Boyd centre field, and Thomas, right field.

They played better ball, by far, this year than the year previous. Their games attracted the attention of base ball writers all over the country, and the "Cuban Giants" were heralded everywhere as marvels of the base ball world. They were not looked upon by the public as freaks, but they were classed as men of talent. They proved to be very shrewd in detecting the inside work and tricks of their opponents, and later would use them to their own advantage.

BEN HOLMES
Captain and Third Baseman of the
first Professional colored team, of Babylon, L. I.

They closed the season of '86 with a grand record made against National League and the leading college teams.

Eighteen hundred and eight-seven saw the launching of a League of Colored Base Ball Clubs. The cities represented were Boston, New York, Philadelphia, Baltimore, Washington, Pittsburgh and Louisville.

The great prominence attained by the Cuban Giants, no doubt, led some people to think that colored base ball, patterned after the National League, with a team in every big league city, would draw the same number of people.

With Walter Brown (now deceased), of Pittsburgh, as president, they opened the season. May 1st, the Resolutes of Boston traveled to Louisville, Ky., a distance of over one thousand miles, to play two games and open the season in Louisville. The Gorhams, of New York, jumped to Pittsburgh, over four hundred miles. Washington and Baltimore, with a short jump of forty miles, were no better after the first series financially, than the other teams. With a schedule calling for two games for members of the League at each city, and a small guarantee with a privilege of half the gate receipts, it was little wonder some of the teams failed to appear for their second engagement.

The League, on the whole, was without substantial backing and consequently did not last a week. But the short time of its existence served to bring out the fact that colored ball players of ability were numerous. The teams, with the exception of the Keystones, of Pittsburgh, and the Gorhams, of New York, were

GEORGE WILLIAMS
Captain and Second Baseman of the
Original Cuban Giants

composed mostly of home talent, so they were not necessarily compelled to disband. With reputations as clubs from the defunct Colored League, they proved to be very good drawing cards in different sections of the country. The Keystones and Gorhams, especially distinguished themselves by later defeating the Cuban Giants.

A notable event this year was the great Western trip of the Cuban Giants, playing Cincinnati, Indianapolis, Wheeling and other teams of the West. They were quite successful on their tour, winning from Cincinnati and Indianapolis, both big league teams. Their last game on the Western trip was played at Pittsburgh with the Keystones (colored), which ended in a victory for the Keystones by 3–2. George Miller, catcher of the Pittsburgh National League, was umpire. Frank Miller and Weldy Walker were in the points for the Keystones, and Parego and Williams for the Giants.

In justice to the "Giants," it can be said that they were badly crippled at the time and consequently did not display their true form.

Another notable event of the Cuban Giants this year was their great game with the Champion Detroit team of the National League. Detroit had their big four, Brouthers, Rowe, Richardson and White; also Hanlon, now manager of the Cincinnatis; the famous Fred Dunlap, Ganzel, Lady Baldwin, Sam Thompson and Charley Bennett.

The Giants played this great aggregation, and Champions of the World to a standstill; they losing out by a fluke. With the score 4–2 against them in the eighth inning, the Detroits,

WILLIAM WHYTE
Pitcher
Original Cuban Giants

by a series of errors, in which luck played a prominent part, managed to forge ahead and win out in the ninth by 6–4. It was a wonderful achievement for the "Giants" to hold a team like the Detroits were at the time down to such a score, as they were considered by all to be the greatest team of sluggers ever gotten together. Too much credit cannot be given Billy Whyte, who pitched for the Cubans, and would have won his game with proper support.

Eighteen hundred and eighty-eight found the Cuban Giants under the management of S. K. Govern and J. M. Bright. Mr. Cook having died during the season of '87.

The Gorhams, of New York, were now the full-fledged rivals of the Cuban Giants in the East. With Nat Collins, John Nelson, Andrew Jackson, Frank Pell, Oscar Jackson, John Evans, Bob Jackson, Vactor and Davis, they were making a great record throughout New York, New Jersey and Connecticut. They beat the Cuban Giants in Newburgh, N. Y., 4–3.

The important event of this year was the base ball tournament held in New York. The prize a silver ball, was donated by J. M. Bright, part owner of the Cuban Giants. The following clubs entered: Cuban Giants, Keystones of Pittsburgh; Gorhams of New York and the Red Stockings of Norfolk, Va. The teams finished in the order named above. The Cuban Giants winning the ball.

The surprise of the meet was the playing of the Keystones. Their only defeats were at the hands of the Cuban Giants; they won every game played with the Gorhams and Red Sox. The

CLARENCE WILLIAMS
Catcher
Original Cuban Giants

Keystones at this time were not professionals. They having one man other than home talent.

The Red Stockings of Norfolk showed up well in the tournament, but luck seemed to be against them.

All their games were hotly contested, but in the closing innings, luck would invariably step in and beat them.

Eighteen hundred and eighty-nine was an important year in colored base ball. The Cuban Giants, with Harrisburg, Norristown, Lebanon, Lancaster, York, Hazleton and the Gorhams, of New York, formed the Pennsylvania League.

While the Cuban Giants and Harrisburg were fighting for the Championship and running neck and neck, the Gorhams were not out of the running by any means. Harrisburg and the Cuban Giants were much surprised and disconcerted during the season by having two straight defeats registered against them at the hands of the colored boys from New York. The fight for the pennant was bitterly contested between the Harrisburg and Giants. When the last game was played, both teams claimed the pennant. Later it was decided in favor of Harrisburg by a few points.

The intense rivalry between the Cubes and Harrisburg in 1889 led to the formation of the Pennsylvania League the next year on a much stronger basis in every particular. A party of gentlemen who backed the Harrisburg of '89 secured the grounds in York, and signing the Cuban Giants placed them in York as representatives of the League. The same bitter rivalry was carried through the Winter into the season of '90 by partisans of the

GEORGE PARAGO
Pitcher
Original Cuban Giants

two teams and when the boys reported in the Spring, they found two of their number missing. To weaken the "Giants" chances for the pennant and to enhance their own, the Harrisburg management had signed C. Williams and F. Grant, of the Cubans. The case of Grant was carried to court as both teams claimed his services for 1890.

The Court decided in favor of Harrisburg. The York management at once signed A. and O. Jackson and White, of the Gorhams. It was quite a race for the lead the first month between York, Harrisburg and Altoona; after which the colored boys gradually pulled away until July, when they were so far in the lead that Harrisburg jumped to the Atlantic League to save them the shame of being left so far behind in a race for the pennant.

It can be said for the management of the Harrisburgs, that although fighting the colored team by every conceivable manner on the ball field, they never drew the color line in any of the League meetings. They would not enter unless their colored player, Frank Grant, was allowed to play.

After the Pennsylvania League disbanded July 5th, the Yorks, colored Monarchs of the Diamond, as J. Monroe Kreider, their Mgr. called them, started on a tour of Pennsylvania playing independent ball until the close of the season. While the original Cuban Giants were playing in York, under new management, J. M. Bright, with a team of new material, was playing under the name of Cuban Giants and doing well. It was also during this year that the first colored professional team in the West was started. They were organized in Lincoln, Neb., and were

ARTHUR THOMAS (Deceased)
Catcher
Original Cuban Giants

Their ages ranging from 22 to 32; every man placed where he was strongest, pitchers and catchers strong in field and at bat, every man a student of the game and experienced, they were a hard team for any club to beat. Their line-up was as follows: Arthur Thomas and Clarence Williams, catchers; Geo. Stovey, Wm. Selden and W. Malone, pitchers; Geo. Williams, first base; Sol White, second base; A. Jackson, third base; F. Grant, short stop; O. Jackson, centre field, and pitchers or catchers in left and right fields.

This year marked the decline of colored base ball in the East for several years. The Lincoln Giants did not reorganize in 1891 their players getting on with white teams in Nebraska and other points in the West.

The Big Gorhams made a record never equaled by any colored team. They played over one hundred games and lost four. They won thirty-nine straight games. New Brunswick beat them the first game, University of Vermont the second, over a month later Glens Falls won from them, and the last was a colored team called the Little Gorhams under the same management as the Big Gorhams.

During this season of 1892 there was only one colored team in the East, the Cuban Giants under the management of J. M. Bright. The season of '91 was so disastrous financially that the Big Gorhams did not re-organize in '92.

While amateur base ball was flourishing in the West, there were no colored professional teams since the Lincoln Giants

WILLIAM MALONE
Pitcher
Original Cuban Giants

called the Lincoln Giants. They had such well-known players as Patterson, now of the Royal Giants; Taylor of Chicago Unions, Miller of the Royal Giants, Maupin, Castone, Reeves, Hughbanks, Lincoln and others.

The Lincoln Giants made a great record during the season of 1890 playing Western League and State League teams: but their backing was not strong enough for a continuance in the business and 1890 saw the last of the Lincoln Giants.

The Lincoln Giants were strong in batteries, hard hitters and fast runners. They were hard to beat unless a strong pitcher was against them.

There were no other colored professional teams at this time except the Colored Monarchs of York (formerly players of original Cuban Giants); Cuban Giants, J. M. Bright, mgr.; Gorhams, of New York, A. Davis, mgr. Up to this time there is no record of any other strictly professional colored teams. This year saw the close of a period in colored base ball which may well be called the money period. From 1885 until the close of 1890, colored base ball flourished. The causes for the change in the condition of things are commented upon in another part of this book.

Eighteen hundred and ninety-one saw quite a change in the line-up by the colored teams of the East. A. Davis, proprietor of the Gorhams, signed every man of the York Monarchs. In addition, he signed C. Williams, F. Grant and Geo. Stovey. This team, now known as the Big Gorhams, was without a doubt one of the strongest teams ever gotten together, white or black.

BENJ. BOYD
Center Fielder
Original Cuban Giants

disbanded, and 1893 and 1894 still saw the one team in the East, the Cuban Giants, although Boston tried for it for a while in '93 but the team only lasted a month.

In 1895 conditions became more encouraging in the East and West, a difference between manager and players of the Cuban Giants. In this year the second colored professional team was organized in the West. It was Grant Johnson in connection with Bud Fowler who conceived the idea of a colored team traveling in a private car and giving street parades on bicycles prior to every game. Grant and Bud found substantial backing for their project in the persons of Messrs Hock, Taylor and Parsons of Adrian, Mich., and in 1895 a new team was launched from whence graduated some of the best colored players of the present time.

With Grant Johnson as Capt. and "Malone," an old Cuban Giant player to steady the youngsters, Johnson and Fowler selected a team of unknown players who made a great record. The private car and bicycles were good advertisements. The team was known as the Page Fence Giants.

The Page Fence Giants was a fine base ball team. They were hard to beat in '95 as their pitchers were among the best and their fielding excellent. With Johnson, Fowler, Patterson, Burns, Brooks, Taylor, Holland, Malone, White, Vandyke, Binga and Miller, the Giants of Adrian were formidable opponents to any team.

In this year can be recorded the first fatality on the ball field in connection with colored base ball. During a game in Hastings, Mich., Brooks, centre fielder of the Page Fence Giants dropped

JOHN FRYE (Deceased)
First Baseman
Original Cuban Giants

while running after a fly ball and never recovered consciousness. He died within an hour. Owing to the weakness of the teams in Michigan and Northern Ohio and the great strength of the Page Fence Giants they (the Giants) had easy sailing during the season and won as they pleased.

The "Chicago Unions" had been the leading amateur colored team of the West since 1886 and during the spring of 1896 they organized to play Sunday games only, with the prairie teams of the city of Chicago. They won every game played during the first season against all kinds of odds, the umpires and crowds in general being against them. Nevertheless they won out and closed the season with a clear record of victories.

They continued playing on the prairies until 1891 when they secured a small ground at 67th street and Langley avenue, playing Sunday games only upon them. They had quite a success for several seasons.

The spring of 1894 found them at 37th and Butler streets where they were more centrally located.

Up to the season of 1896, the team played as amateurs only playing the crack amateur clubs of Chicago, but during 1896 under the management of Messrs. Peters and Leland they branched out as an independent professional team playing every Sunday in Chicago and during the week touring the States of Indiana, Illinois, Wisconsin, Michigan and Iowa: meeting all the professional organizations throughout that county.

Summing up the records of the club during the first twelve seasons of its existence, they made an enviable record by playing

HARRY JOHNSON
Utility man
Original Cuban Giants

731 games. They won 613 and lost 118 and tied 12 which gave them a percentage of .814 for the twelve years.

For the last few years the Unions have been under the management of W. S. Peters, F. Leland having organized the Leland Giants of Chicago.

The Unions have given to the base ball world some of the best ball players in the profession. In the early years of the Unions, "Hopkins," a pitcher was the star of the West, but later gave away to Holland, Buckner, Horn and other ambitious youngsters who are still in the game and doing fine work.

The Unions have produced such players as Hyde, Moore, Holland, Buckner, Horn, Monroe, Jones, Wyatt, Barton and others of note in the colored profession.

The Unions have always been hard hitters and good fielders. Their fault seemed to lie in the lack of interest taken in the fine points of the game.

With their hitting and fielding ability coupled with speed on the bases they would have been unbeatable.

In the East there was a new team called the Cuban X-Giants, under the management of E. B. Lamar, Jr., of New York.

Colored base ball was again at a stand-still in the East and there was nothing of importance to chronicle until 1899. Then came the trip of the Cuban X-Giants in 1897 when they played Chicago, St. Louis, Louisville and Cincinnati. That was the longest trip ever taken by any colored club in America.

In 1899 the Page Fence Giants of Adrian, Michigan, were stationed in Chicago at Thirty-ninth and Wentworth avenue.

JOHN M. BRIGHT
Manager
Genuine Cuban Giants

They were then called the Columbia Giants and were under the management of John W. Patterson. The Columbia Giants with their additional pitcher, Buckner, from the Chicago Unions, were stronger in points at that time than any other colored team. Wilson, Miller, and Buckner formed a trio of twirlers hard to duplicate. Burns and Johnson, catchers; Johnson, Jr., first base; C. Grant, second base; B. Binga third base; G. Johnson, short stop; and Captain Patterson, left field; Barton, centre field, and Reynolds right field. The "Giants" started with good substantial backing having behind them the Columbia Club, an organization composed of Chicago's best business and professional men. Their grounds at Thirty-ninth street and Wentworth avenue were nicely located and their uniforms consisting of a traveling uniform of gray material and a home uniform of white were of the finest. Of the Columbia Giants, it can be said, they were the finest and best equipped colored team that was ever in the business.

The Columbia Giants in opposition to the Unions drew well on Sundays, but their games away from home were not successful financially. In this year there were the Cuban X-Giants and Genuine Cuban Giants in the East, the Red Stockings of Norfolk, Va. in the South and the Chicago Unions and Columbia Giants in the West. Five colored professional base ball teams.

The same teams were still in existence in 1900. Nothing of importance happening in colored base ball this year. The teams of the East were doing well financially while in the West, the teams were holding their own.

"POP" WATKINS
Captain and original Coacher
Genuine Cuban Giants

Nineteen hundred and one saw quite a change in Western base ball circles, the facts of which are chronicled in another part of this book.

In 1902 the Philadelphia Giants, the present Colored Champions, were organized. Harry Smith, base ball writer of the Philadelphia Tribune, conceived the idea of a professional team to represent Philadelphia. So he, in connection with H. Walter Schlichter, of the Philadelphia Item, and the writer, organized the team which are known as the Colored World's Champions. The team as then composed was as follows: Clarence Williams, c.; Wm. Bell, Chas. (Kid) Carter, and John Nelson, pitchers; Harry Smith, first base; Frank Grant, second base; Sol White, short stop; John Hill, third base; Andrew Payne, left field; John Manning, centre field. Like any team during their first year, the changes in their line-up were many, but they played good ball and were very popular.

From 1903 until 1906 there was nothing of importance occurring, other than championship contests, which are noted in another part of the book.

In 1906 a new team appeared in the field. J. W. Connor, colored, of Brooklyn, owner of the Royal Cafe, organized a team and called them the Royal Giants. They are now managed and captained by Grant Johnson, of Page Fence and Columbia Giants fame, and they are now one of the leading colored clubs of the country.

The year of 1906 was notable in colored base ball circles. There seemed to be a base ball epidemic, especially in the East. Within a radius of one hundred miles there were no less than nine

J. GARCIA (Deceased)
Catcher
Genuine Cuban Giants

professional colored base ball teams, viz.: Philadelphia Giants, Cuban X-Giants, Genuine Cuban Giants, Royal Giants, Quaker Giants of N. Y., Wilmington Giants, New York Giants, Baltimore Giants, of Newark and Keystone Giants, of Philadelphia. There were also two teams from Cuba: Cuban Stars and Havana Stars. With the forming of the International League, some of the teams managed to last until after the Fourth of July. The Quaker Giants, Wilmington Giants and Havana team disbanded in the latter part of July.

The season ended with the Philadelphia Giants, Cuban X-Giants, Royal Giants and Genuine Giants battling for supremacy in the East, and the Chicago Unions and Leland Giants in the West. The Royal Giants, of Brooklyn were considerably strengthened by the addition of Patterson, Johnson, Jr., Monroe and Wright, of the defunct Quaker Giants. The Cuban X-Giants, with Buckner and Barton, of the Quaker Giants, and Gatewood and Petway, of the Leland Giants of Chicago, were far stronger at the close of the season than in the beginning. The Cuban Giants added Earl, a pitcher, to their line-up, and the "Phillies" grabbed Francis, third baseman of the defunct Wilmington Giants.

The International League, with Freihofer, president, and John A. O'Rourke, secretary, organized with the following members: Cuban X-Giants, Quaker Giants, of New York; Cuban Stars, Havanas, of Cuba; Philadelphia Professionals and Riverton-Palmyra Athletics. Later the Wilmington Giants took the place of one of the Cuban teams, and the Philadelphia Giants joined the League in August, taking the place of the Quaker Giants.

The Philadelphia Giants won the pennant and a beautiful cup donated by President Freihofer. The deciding game was played on the American League grounds, Philadelphia, September 3d, Labor Day, before 10,000 people, the largest crowd of spectators that ever attended a base ball game between colored teams.

This virtually ended the season of colored base ball and settled the question of premiership among the teams of the East and the West also.

The Philadelphia Giants, by the hardest struggle of their career, still maintained the name of World's Colored Champion by winning a majority of games played with every colored team in the East and winning also from the Chicago Unions and Leland Giants of the West. By playing three games in one day and winning all they established a wonderful record. On September 30th they met the Royal Giants in a morning game at Elizabeth, N. J., and defeated them 6–1. In the afternoon they met the Cuban X-Giants at Brighton Oval, Brooklyn, and defeated them 5–2, and later in the day played Brighton Athletic Club and beat them 6–2. This day, September 30th, marked the close of twenty years of professional Colored Base Ball. Taking lessons from the past, there seems to be nothing but the brightest prospects for great advancement in the future.

CHASE LYONS
Pitcher
Genuine Cuban Giants

Championship Contests

Championship contests of a local nature are as a rule more bitterly fought than others of a different character. There will not be found the same feeling displayed during a contest when the teams are from distant parts of the country as when there is a local contest.

When teams travel to a far section of the country to meet for a championship struggle, there is always given to the visitors a most hearty welcome. With a friendly grasp of the hand and a "Pleased to meet you" and a "I hope we will have a good game," style of greeting, they are escorted to their hotel by the home manager and self appointed committees of "fans" who desire to show visitors a good time while they are in the city. The same good cheer and friendship is carried on the field and while the games are invariably well contested and interesting, they lack that never-say-die spirit that always creeps into a struggle between teams of the same section of the country, or two teams battling for prestige in an immediate locality.

Situations, as described above, occur yearly in colored base ball, East and West, and go far to keep up the interest among colored patrons of the National game.

The first bitter struggle between colored rivals in the base ball world occurred in 1887. The Cuban Giants, of Trenton, and the Gorhams, of New York, were the first colored teams to clash on the diamond for what may be termed local supremacy. Although located in and around New York, they played to large and

CUBAN X-GIANTS Season, 1905.

appreciative crowds. Their success financially and from a playing sense was phenomenal. The Gorhams, undaunted, hooked up with the Cuban Giants at every opportunity and by hard earnest endeavor played them to a standstill upon all occasions, until at last victory crowned their efforts.

It was at Newburgh, N. Y., when after many futile efforts to gain a victory over the "Giants" the Gorhams, by main grit and nervy ball playing managed to win out in a game replete with sensational fielding and daring acts on the bases. With Nelson and B. Jackson of the Gorhams, opposed to Parago and Williams for the Giants, the game was bitterly contested until the last inning, when O. Jackson of the Gorhams scored the winning run on an infield hit by mixing it up with Williams at the plate, Williams dropping the ball. The score was 4 to 3.

In 1888 the games played by the Cuban Giants, Keystones of Pittsburgh, Gorhams of New York and Red stockings of Norfolk, for the silver ball and the colored Championship has been fully commented upon in the first part of the book.

In 1889 the Gorhams and Cuban Giants, both members of the Pennsylvania League, played regular league schedule games. At Easton, Pa., the home of the Gorhams, the Giants and Gorhams met to play their first league series of the season.

These games were hotly contested. Malone and Whyte pitched for the Giants; Miller and Nelson for the Gorhams. The series went to the Gorhams, they won both games by the same score, 4–3.

There were no other championship games between colored teams until 1896 when the Cuban X-Giants went West to play the Page Fence Giants, of Adrian, Michigan. (Although in 1894, the Cuban Giants took their first trip west to play the Chicago Unions, the two games played were of minor importance as the Unions at that time were amateurs and somewhat easy for the Giants.) The colored championship was not involved in this contest between the Cuban X-Giants and the Page Fence Giants, as the Cuban X-Giants had never met the Genuine Cuban Giants of the East nor had the Page Fence Giants met the Chicago Unions of the West, but the games were played as though the world's premiership rested on the outcome. The agreement called for fifteen games. The team winning eight games of the fifteen to be declared winner of the series and a championship. The Page Fence Giants, after the second game of the series, won as they pleased. The Cuban X-Giants lacked condition, and after the second game were as bad, physically, as a team in spring practice. The boys from Adrian were in the pink of condition and played great ball. Of the first fifteen games played the Page Fence Giants won ten and the Cuban X-Giants five.

The Page Fence Giants were given beautiful medals by their manager and also an extra compensation for winning the series.

The first championship games in the East since the Cuban Giant – Gorham struggle took place at the Weehauken grounds in the fall of 1897 between the Genuine Cuban Giants and

E. B. LAMAR, Jr.
Manager and Owner
Cuban X-Giants

the Cuban X-Giants. The games were played three successive Sundays and resulted in two out of three for the Cuban X-Giants which gave them undisputed right to the Colored Championship of the East.

In 1899 the first real championship games between the East and West were played. The Cuban X-Giants the real colored champions of the East journeyed to Chicago to play a series of games with the "Unions" of Chicago. The "Unions" were stronger this year than at any time since their organization. Footes, Jackson, Horn, Holland, Moore, Hopkins, Hyde, Monroe, W. Jones and Bert Jones were the men that composed the Unions. The Cuban X-Giants had Williams, Selden, Nelson, Howard, Wilson, F. Grant, A. Jackson, White, W. Jackson and Jordan. Fourteen games were played in and around Chicago, the crowds on several occasions being enormous. The games were hotly contested all through the series but the superior hitting of the Cuban X-Giants won for them the title of Champions. They won nine of fourteen games played.

It was in this year that the Page Fence Giants of Adrian, Mich., moved to Chicago and played under the name of the Columbia Giants. While Cuban X-Giants and Unions were playing their series, the Columbia Giants were issuing all sorts of challenges to the winner or the loser. The result was the acceptance by the Unions and the Cuban X-Giants also.

The Union and Columbia Giants had long been at loggerheads owing to the invasion of Chicago by the Page Fence Giants and the Unions heretofore would not entertain a proposition relating

RAY WILSON
Captain
Cuban X-Giants

to a series with the Giants, out of consideration for the public, the Unions agreed to play a series of five games for the local championship. The Columbia Giants, by their long string of victories during the season were favorites in the betting at ten to seven. The Unions were not without a following and were backed heavily at the prevailing odds. The rivalry was intense and spectators and players were worked to a high pitch of excitement.

The Columbia Giants were stronger in the box than the Unions and made less errors in their fielding. These qualifications won for the Columbia Giants the local Championship of Chicago and a big bunch of money. Of the five games played, the "Unions" did not win a game.

The Columbia Giants now turned their attention to the Cuban X-Giants, of New York. A series of games was arranged between the two teams and was played in Chicago and in towns in Michigan. Eleven games were played. The Cuban X-Giants won the series by seven to four.

Nineteen hundred was a great year for the two Western clubs from a playing standpoint. The Cuban X-Giants, who had been winning from the Unions so consistently year after year, made their annual trip to Chicago for another series with the same team. The Unions won from the "Giants" for the first time in their career. While the Unions were thrashing the Cuban X-Giants, of New York, the Columbia Giants were walloping the Genuine Cuban Giants, of New York.

The two Western teams won as they pleased this year.

JOHN NELSON
Pitcher
Cuban X-Giants, 1896 to 1902

During two season's following, 1901 and 1902, there were no championship contests in the colored professional ranks.

In nineteen hundred and three, there was the Algona Brownies, of Algona, Ia., a team composed of former Unions and Columbia Giant players, playing the Unions for the championship of the West and the Giants, of Philadelphia, playing the Cuban X-Giants for the premiership of the East.

The Algona Brownies with Geo. Johnson, B. Jones, Horn, Ball, Moore and other noted players, beat the Unions in a series of games which were noted for lack of enthusiasm.

The Philadelphia Giants and the Cuban X-Giants, after two years of squabbling, challenges and counter challenges, got together and arranged to play for the colored championship of the world.

These games were of the utmost importance and were fought with the bitterest feeling at every stage of the series. Eight games were to have been played but the Cuban X-Giants won five of the first seven, thereby winning the championship.

It would have been a hard matter to pick the winner before the series, especially by form in previous games or by the lineup of the nines. Both were strong in the pitching department and good with the stick. The Philadelphia Giants were confident of winning as they had some of the hardest hitters of the colored profession in Robert Footes, William Bell, Charles Carter, Harry Buckner, Sol White, Frank Grant, William Monroe, William Binga, John Patterson, John Nelson and William Evans but the pitching of Foster backed by the

JOHN HILL
Short Stop
Cuban X-Giants

superior work of his team-mates won a clean cut victory for the Cuban X-Giants.

The winning team was composed of the following players: Clarence Williams, Robert Jordan, Andrew Foster, Dan McClellan, James Robinson, Ed Wilson, Ray Wilson, Charles Grant, John Hill, Grant Johnson, William Jackson, Andrew Payne and William Smith.

Of the games played Foster won four, McClellan one, Carter one, and Bell one.

The Phillies were out-played in all departments of the game and did not show the form which they displayed in the earlier part of the season.

The features of this contest were the pitching of Foster, who won every game he pitched (four), and the great hitting of Jordan, who hit at a .560 clip during the series.

In 1904, the Cuban X-Giants and Philadelphia Giants again hooked up in another struggle for the Championship. The Phillies, owing to dissension in the team in 1903, were far from being satisfied with their defeat of that year and claimed that with proper harmony in their ranks, they could turn the trick on their much hated rivals.

This Championship series consisted of three games, which were played in Atlantic City. Both players and spectators were worked to the highest pitch of excitement. Never in the annals of colored baseball did two nines fight for supremacy as these teams fought.

W. S. PETERS
Owner and Manager
Chicago Unions

Everything known to baseball was done by both nines to win, but the Phillies by the nerviest kind of ball playing, and the best kind of pitching by Foster, who was now with the Phillies, won two out of three and the proud title of Colored Champions of the World.

The Philadelphia Giants, on paper, seemed to be outclassed when matched with the Cuban X-Giants this season. Below is the personnel of the teams that met in Atlantic City:

Phila. Giants		Cuban X-Giants
R. Footes	Catcher	C. Williams
G. Johnson, Jr.	Catcher	R. Jordan
A. Foster	Pitcher	D. McClellan
C. Carter	Pitcher	A. Ball
W. Bell	Pitcher	J. Robinson
W. Horn	Pitcher	H. Buckner
S. White	First Base	R. Jordan
C. Grant	Second Base	J. Patterson
W. Monroe	Shortstop	G. H. R. Johnson
J. Hill	Third Base	J. Smith
P. Hill	Left Field	W. Jackson
A. Payne	Centre Field	H. Moore
W. Bell	Right Field	W. Smith

In stick work the Philadelphia Giants were supposed to be weak. The Cuban X-Giants were outbattled by fifty-seven points. The Phillies having an average of .201 and the Cubans .144. The Philadelphia Giants played a better fielding game.

HARRY HYDE
Captain
Chicago Unions

Their fielding average for the series being .944 while the Cubes' average was .918.

The Cubes stole the most bases, they having seven to their credit, while the Phillies stole five.

Patterson and Grant Johnson did the hitting for the Cuban X-Giants. Patterson leading with an average of .346.

Foster in two games led the Phillies with an average of .400. He was followed by Geo. Johnson with .352.

The features of this contest were the pitching of Foster, who pitched two of the three games, winning both and striking out eighteen men in the first game and letting the Cubes down with two hits the third game, and the hitting and base running of Patterson, he making two home runs during the series and stealing four bases in one game.

The Philadelphia Giants beat the All-Cubans, of Cuba, three of five games this year, which gave them the title of Champions of Cuba.

In 1905 the colored teams of the East could not come to any agreement, and no series of any kind were arranged.

In the West, the Chicago Union Giants and the Leland Giants were having a battle royal in Chicago for the Championship of the West.

The Union Giants, with Geo. Wilson and Geo. Johnson of the Renville, Minn., team as a battery managed to tie the Leland Giants in the fifth game of the contest, which left the series standing even at two and two.

DAVID WYATT
Outfielder
Chicago Unions

During 1906 there was a four-cornered fight between the Philadelphia Giants, Cuban X-Giants, and Royal Giants, of Brooklyn, and Wilmington Giants, for the honors of the colored base ball world. The result of the games played left no doubt as to where the honor belonged. The Philadelphia Giants though badly crippled the entire season, won a majority of games from every colored team they played and clearly demonstrated their superiority over all competitors for colored base ball supremacy.

Of the five games played with the Wilmington Giants, the Philadelphia Giants won four and tied one. The Royal Giants of Brooklyn and the Phillies, played seventeen games, the Phillies won eleven and lost six. Of the fifteen games played with the Cuban X-Giants, the Phillies won ten and lost five, making a total of 37 games played by the Phillies against the colored teams of which they won 25, lost 11 and tied one, giving them a percentage of .694 against .306 for their opponents.

The success of the Philadelphia Giants of 1906 was due no doubt, to their gameness. A gamer gang of ball players never stepped on a diamond. More or less crippled throughout the season, they played the hardest teams with the same spirit as the weak ones. When the other teams were strengthening by adding stars to their lineup, the Phillies were weakening by accidents and sickness. When the odds against them were greatest, they seemed the more determined and their nonchalant air bred a personality that told their opponents they would have to play ball or they could not win.

The following defy was sent to the winner of the world's series between the Athletics and New Yorks, by Manager Schlichter, of the Philadelphia Giants, through the New York press.

WANTS TO MATCH THE GIANTS FOR THE CHAMPIONSHIP

Walter Schlichter, the well known sporting editor of the "Item," who is also the manager of the Philadelphia Giants, the colored base ball team, is out with a very novel proposition and one that will no doubt startle the whole base ball world. Slick (everybody calls him Slick) took hold of the bunch of colored ball players a couple of years ago and by continually weeding them out and introducing new blood he has made them one of the strongest, wide awake ball teams in the country. Slick has also shown his ability as a press agent and booster by continually advertising the team till they are now known to everyone who takes even the slightest interest in baseball. This has made the Philadelphia Giants one of the best cards in baseball and there is a constant demand for their services seven days a week.

The Philadelphia Giants have won their way to the top and are now the recognized champion colored ball team of the world. Now Schlichter shows that he is ambitious, for he wants to match his team against the winners of the white championship, be it either in the National or the American league. Schlichter wants to play a series of three or five games and thus decide who can play base ball the best – the white or the black American.

At first glance it might seem as if Schlichter's only idea was with the view of making money and that it was not to be taken seriously.

But a careful investigation of the playing record of the Philadelphia Giants will show that they have earned the right to play against the best white teams for they can put an article of base ball that is as good as the best and at any stage of the game they could make either the Athletics or the New York National Leaguers, hustle to win out. Of course, there is a possibility of the colored men winning and that would be distasteful to many followers of the white team, but true sport recognizes no color nor clan and it should always be, may the best man win.

It is to be hoped for the sake of the sport that Schlichter's challenge for a series of games will be accepted by the winners of the white championship. Such a series of games played in Philadelphia and New York would prove a tremendous attraction and be well worth the trouble, for it would mean a big gate for the club owners and a nice wad of money for the players. Here's luck to Slick and hoping that he can get on his championship series.

ROBERT JACKSON
Catcher
Chicago Unions

"The Roadside"
514 S. 15th Street
PHILADELPHIA, PENNA.

A. S. JONES, Prop.

CALL AND SEE ME
Wines and Liquors

"The Item"

Sixty years of continuous success.

Sworn circulation for 1906

Daily average circulation, 248,076
Sunday   "   "   242,627

All the sporting news covered in detail.

Daily Item - - - 1c
Sunday Item - - - 1c

"The Item" leads. Others follow

===

**Main Office: 28 S. 7th Street,
PHILADELPHIA, PA.**

Notable Feats of Colored Pitchers

Of the great feats performed by colored pitchers the game in which Billy Whyte, of the Original Cuban Giants, twirled against the famous Detroit team of 1887, was one of the most noteworthy. Whyte was unexpectedly called upon to face the greatest team of sluggers in the history of the game, and for a time had them at his mercy. Detroit won out in the last two innings by the ragged fielding of the Giants. Whyte was one of the best colored pitchers the game ever saw. Below is the score by innings of the Cuban Giants-Detroit game of 1887:

										R.	H.	E.
Detroit	0	0	1	0	1	0	0	2	2–	6	6	0
Cuban Giants	0	1	0	2	0	0	1	0	0–	4	8	4

Batteries–Conway and Ganzel for Detroit; Whyte and Williams for Cuban Giants.

George Stovey struck out twenty-two of the Bridgeport (Conn.) Eastern League team in 1886 and lost his game.

Dan McClellan, of the Philadelphia Giants, is the only pitcher of color who has the distinction of blanking a team without a hit or run or a man reaching first. McClellan accomplished this feat against the York, Pa., team in 1903.

York, Pa., July 17–Before McClellan's masterly pitching the Penn Park Athletic Club today was shut out without a single player reaching first base and only 27 batting in the game.

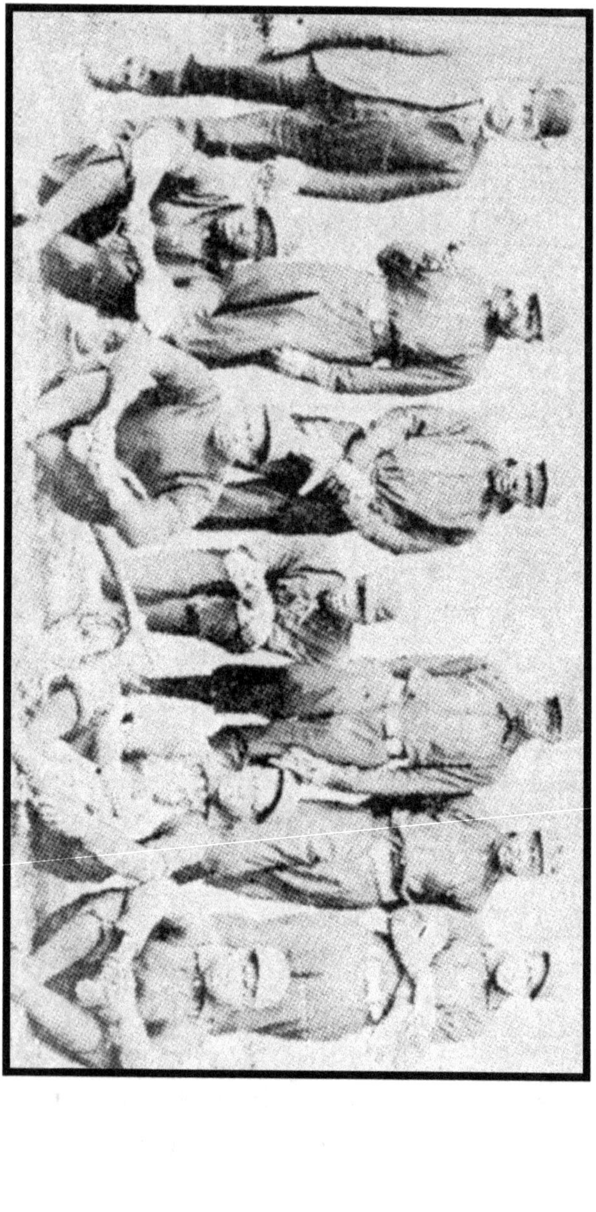

RED STOCKINGS, of Norfolk, Va. Season, 1904.

		R.	H.	E.
Penn Park 0 0 0 0 0 0 0 0 0–		0	0	4
Cuban X-Giants 0 0 0 2 3 0 0 0 x–		5	12	6

Batteries-Hilbert and Smith; McClellan and Williams. Umpire-Sturgen. Time, 1.05. Attendance, 600.

McClellan pitched a great game in 1905 against the Newark Eastern League team keeping hits well scattered and shutting them out 4 to 0.

NEWARK.

	AB.	R.	H.	O.	A.	E.
Cockman, 3b	4	0	3	2	2	0
Murphy, cf	3	0	0	1	0	0
Jons, lf	3	0	1	4	0	0
Dillard, rf	3	0	1	0	0	0
Gatins, ss	4	0	0	3	6	2
Connors, 1b	4	0	1	11	1	0
Mahling, 2b	4	0	1	2	2	0
Latimer, c	4	0	1	3	1	0
McPherson, p	4	0	0	1	3	2
*Skopec	1	0	0	0	0	0
Totals	34	0	8	27	15	4

*Batted for McPherson in ninth.

PHILADELPHIA GIANTS.

	AB.	R.	H.	O.	A.	E.
Grant, 2b	4	1	0	5	3	0
Hill, lf	4	1	2	4	0	0
Monroe, 3b	4	1	1	2	1	0

Kimball's Anti-Rheumatic Ring

A speedy and permanent cure for rheumatism, neuralgia, sciatica, gout, paralysis and all other diseases where a general warming, quickening, strengthening and equalization of the circulation is required.

For sale by ——————

H. D. LECATO
Room 712 Girard Trust Building
Broad and Chestnut Sts.,
PHILADELPHIA, PA.

Main Office
1-3 Union Square,
New York City

Johnson, ss	3	1	0	2	7	0
Moore, cf	4	0	2	2	0	0
McClellan, p	4	0	0	0	1	0
Foster, rf	4	0	0	0	0	0
White, 1b	4	0	0	8	0	0
Devoe, c	3	0	0	4	0	0
Totals	34	4	5	27	12	0

Newarks......... 0 0 0 0 0 0 0 0 0–0
Phila. Giants.... 1 0 3 0 0 0 0 0 0–4

Batteries—McPherson and Latimer. McClellan and Devoe. Umpire, Mr. Snyder.

Foster, of the Philadelphia Giants, from his consistent work of the past four seasons, has earned the reputation of being one of the best colored pitchers the game has produced.

Foster has pitched several no hits games, and has struck out as high as 18 men in a single game against such teams as the Trenton Y.M.C.A. of 1904 and the Cuban X-Giants of 1904.

Below is the tabulated scores of three games in which Foster's work was remarkable.

CAMDEN.

	R.	H.	O.	A.	E.
Meehan, cf	0	0	2	0	0
Miller, c	0	0	2	0	0
Zollers, ss	0	0	4	5	2
Slack, 1b	0	0	14	1	1
Verga, 3b	0	0	0	2	0
Cross, 2b	0	0	3	0	0
MacMannis, lf	0	0	1	1	0

PHILADELPHIA GIANTS. Champions. Season, 1905.

Brown, p	0	0	0	7	0
Robinson, rf	0	0	1	1	0
Totals	0	0	27	18	3

PHILADELPHIA GIANTS.

	R.	H.	O.	A.	E.
Grant, 2b	0	1	1	2	0
Johnson, ss	0	0	0	0	0
Hill, lf	1	1	2	0	0
Monroe, ss	1	0	2	3	0
Moore, cf	1	1	2	0	0
Foster, p	0	0	2	5	0
Bowman, rf	0	1	1	1	0
Washington, c	0	0	5	0	0
Thomas, 1b	0	0	12	1	1
Totals	3	4	27	12	0

Camden	0	0	0	0	0	0	0	0	0	0–0
Giants	0	1	0	0	2	0	0	0	0	0–3

Two base hits—Hill Bowman. Sacrifice hits—Brown, Foster. Left on bases—Camden, 3; Philadelphia Giants, 3. Struck out—By Brown, 2; by Foster, 5. Bases on balls—By Brown, 1; by Foster, 2. Time—1.30. Umpire—Osborn.

PHILA. GIANTS VS. CUBAN X-GIANTS.

Atlantic City, Sept. 1, 1904.

PHILADELPHIA GIANTS.

	R.	H.	O.	A.	E.
Grant, 2b	1	1	0	1	1
Monroe, ss	1	0	1	1	1
White, 1b	0	0	5	0	0
Payne, lf	2	3	1	1	0
P. Hill, cf	1	1	1	0	0
Johnson, c	1	1	19	0	0
Foster, p	1	3	0	0	0
J. Hill, 3b	0	1	0	1	0
Footes, rf	1	0	0	1	0
Totals	8	10	27	5	1

CUBAN X-GIANTS.

	R.	H.	O.	A.	E.
Johnson, ss	0	0	3	3	0
Patterson, 2b	2	2	4	2	0
Jordan, 1b	1	1	8	0	2
Moore, cf	0	1	1	0	3
Jackson, lf	0	1	1	0	0
Buckner, 1b	1	1	5	1	0
Smith, 3b	0	0	1	1	0
Williams, c	0	0	4	3	0
McClellan, p	0	0	0	2	0
Ball, p	0	1	0	0	0
Totals	4	7	27	12	5

Batteries—Foster and Johnson; Ball and McClellan and Williams. Struck out by Foster, 18; by Ball, 2; by McClellan, 2. Umpires, Adams and Agnew.

PHILA. GIANTS VS. CUBAN X-GIANTS.
Atlantic City, Sept. 3d, 1904.

PHILADELPHIA GIANTS.

	R.	H.	O.	A.	E.
Grant, 2b	1	1	1	7	0
White, 1b	1	2	11	1	3
Monroe, ss	0	0	2	2	0
Payne, lf	0	0	0	0	0
P. Hill, cf	0	0	0	0	0
Johnson, c	0	1	7	1	0
Foster, p	1	1	1	3	0
J. Hill, 3b	0	1	2	3	1
Bell, rf	1	0	3	0	0
Totals	4	6	27	17	3

CUBAN X-GIANTS.

	R.	H.	O.	A.	E.
Johnson, ss	1	1	3	0	1
Patterson, 2b	1	1	3	2	0
Jordan, 1b	0	0	9	1	0
Moore, cf	0	0	2	0	2
Buckner, rf	0	0	1	0	0
Jackson, lf	0	0	1	0	0
J. Smith, 3b	0	0	1	3	0

H. WALTER SCHLICHTER
(Slick)
Sporting Editor "Philadelphia Item"
President, The National Association of Colored Baseball Clubs of the United States and Cuba.
President and manager of the Philadelphia Giants B. B. and A. A., Inc.

Williams, c	0	0	6	1	0
McClellan, p	0	0	0	2	0
Totals	2	2	27	9	3

Batteries—Foster and Johnson: McClellan and Williams. Struck out—By Foster, 5: by McClellan, 3. Umpires—Adams and Meber.

Horn, pitching for the Philadelphia Giants, shut the Oxford, Pa., team out without a hit or run in 1904.

Hopkins, of the Chicago Unions, has frequently struck out twelve and fifteen men in games with strong amateur and semi-professional teams of Chicago.

George Wilson, of Columbia Giants fame, has pitched some wonderful games against the strongest teams of the West. Wilson is one of the most difficult men to hit among the colored pitchers. He is a bronzed "Waddell" when right.

Other pitchers that have done remarkable work and are considered to be present day stars, are: Billy Holland, of the Royal Giants; H. E. Buckner; John Davis, Leland Giants; Gatewood, Cuban X-Giants; Carter and Merritt of the Royal Giants; Sampson and Best of Genuine Cuban Giants; Washington, of Jacksonville, Fla.; Bowman, Philadelphia Giants; Foster, Philadelphia Giants, and others.

CHAS. Kid CARTER
Pitcher
Philadelphia Giants, 1902 to 1905

Colored Base Ball as a Profession

There is nothing like protecting the rights of the owners of base ball teams and while the ball players generally work in the opposite directions, they move under a false star and are only temporarily benefitted. The owner of a base ball team is in the business to make money for years to come, while the player is in the game to make the biggest rake off in the quickest time, never knowing just when he will have hard luck and fail to keep up a hot pace.

The colored ball player should always look before he leaps. He should remember that, although possessing the ability in every particular of the white ball player, he is not in a position to demand the same salary as his white brother, as the difference in the receipts of their respective games are decidedly in favor of the latter; thousands attending games of the whites to hundreds of the blacks. Leaving out the colored stars of the International League of 1887, the aggregate salaries for colored ball players, amounted to a little over $5,500 for a season of $5\frac{1}{2}$ months. 1906, the banner year for colored base ball, when the number of teams is considered, with no less than 150 ball players employed in the professional ranks, they drew over $70,000 in salaries for the season, an average of $466 per man. An increase of over 785 per cent, from 1886 to 1907, or an average of $39\frac{1}{4}$ per cent increase each year.

These figures, in comparison, are expressly low to the salaries received and the business done by players and owners of

ANDREW (Rube) FOSTER
Pitcher
Philadelphia Giants, 1904 to 1907

white teams. Statistics of 1906 show the two major leagues alone paying over $600,000 per season to more than 300 ball players. While the minor leagues pay over $2,000,000 to 3,500 players.

These figures give the major league players an average of $2,000 per man for a season's work; and the minor league players $571 per man. The disparity in the salary of a major league player and a colored player is enormous, especially when it is taken into consideration that, were it not for color, many would be playing in the big league for $2,000, or more per season instead of less than $500 per season. As it is, they receive less than the minor league player.

Base ball is a legitimate profession. As much so as any other vocation, and should be fostered by owners and players alike. It is indisputably a masculine game, demanding all manly qualities and powers to the extreme. It is immune from attacks from all critics. From a scientific standpoint it outclasses all other American games. It should be taken seriously by the colored player, as honest efforts with his great ability will open an avenue in the near future wherein he may walk hand-in-hand with the opposite race in the greatest of all American games – base ball.

CHARLES GRANT
Second Baseman
Philadephia Giants

G. GRANT WILLIAMS

OUR ONLY COLORED DAILY PAPER
The Philadelphia Tribune
DAILY and WEEKLY

CHRIS. J. PERRY, *Publisher*.
G. GRANT WILLIAMS, *City Editor*.

Published every afternoon at
717 Sansom St., Philadelphia, Pa.

The best Medium for advertising when you want to reach the people.

J. P. HILL
Left Fielder
Philadelphia Giants

Managers' Troubles

The tribulations of a manager of the base ball team, especially a colored team, are known only to those who have inside knowledge of the game and are familiar with what a base ball manager has to contend.

To deal with the question from an independent stand-point, it is found more difficult to handle a team in that respect than when a member of a league, under the National agreement. Rules laid down by league teams are easily enforced; from the fact that players in the minor organizations have aspirations to shine as stars in the major leagues and consequently cannot afford a reckless disregard of the rules to compel them to keep in condition for first-class ball playing. Once in the big league they have a horror of being relegated to the minors, which creates a greater respect for the rules.

In this day and time, when colored base ball teams are numerous and each striving for supremacy, the colored manager's path is not one of sunshine. With twelve or fourteen men under his command, twelve or fourteen different minds and dispositions to control and centre on the intricate points of play, with no National League of base ball clubs behind the rules and regulations, with the many complaints of players and threats of quitting ringing in his ears day after day, he passes many a sleepless night and will often ask for that "Patience he needs."

DAN McCLELLAN
Pitcher
Philadelphia Giants

To guard against such contingencies, managers, should be careful in selecting players to compose a team. A player of mediocre ability who is a willing and hard worker and easily handled, is far better in every respect to a team than one of rare ability with so much self-importance as to create a feeling of antipathy among his fellow players.

It will be found that 80 per cent of these self-important players think so well of their individual reputations, that an error or misplay on their part during a game is liable to make them lose their nerve.

It is the man with the nerve that gets there, but in base ball there are two kinds of nerve. One kind is on the outside and the other on the inside. For a winner, the inside nerve is the best every time. A "four flusher" will make all kinds of noise with his mouth, but when it comes to a test on the ball field, will develop a "yellow streak" a yard long. The ball player with the nerve on the inside does but little talking about what he is going to do, but just watch the man when it comes to the game depending on quick action and he is invariably there.

Managers should possess gray matter and have up-to-date ideas. They should acquire a full understanding of the game and strive to instil it into the heads of his players. There is a general weakness among colored players that mitigates to a great extent against their success on the diamond, that is, their lack of knowledge and understanding of the playing rules. The rules should be thoroughly understood as games have been won and lost where the deciding play depended on the interpretation of a rule.

EMMETT BOWMAN
Pitcher
Philadelphia Giants

They should aim to blend the team into a highly polished and magnificent machine. The play itself is a science, if that term may be applied to sport. Compared to town ball or other old fashioned games, it suggests the present day harvesting engine and its prototype, the scythe.

The attitude of the spectators, or as they are popularly called "fans" has changed at about the same rate as the game. Formerly they were content with being amused and the game developed comedians like Abe Harrison and Bill Joyner. But now they demand faultless play. Genuine diversion is as scarce as the green carnation. Rugged, callous, fearless though he be, the player seldom volunteers any original fun-making on the field, or on the coaching-line, lest the "fans" take it amiss.

Not that the spectator is unwilling to be amused! He goes to the game with that hope and intention – so eager for amusement. Indeed, that if a player somersaults on a wet field, or another doffs his cap with a sly, unwonted grimace, after making a great catch. It provokes Heaven-splitting laughter.

On the other hand, mighty and bitter is the reward of wrath visited upon one who by lack of vigilance, activity or quickness brings disaster upon his team.

The funny man in colored base ball is becoming extinct. Where every man on a team would do a funny stunt during a game back in the eighties and early nineties, now will be found only one or two on a team who essays to amuse the spectators of the present day. Monroe, third baseman of the Royal Giants of Brooklyn is the leading fun-maker of the colored profession of to-day. His comic sayings and actions while on the field, together with his ability as a fielder, hitter and runner has earned for him a great reputation as a ball player. Joyner, of Chicago, draws a salary for fun-making alone. Pop Watkins, Gordon and Best of the Genuine Cuban Giants, are the other present day comedians of the diamond.

The majority of colored ball players are now carefully watching the scientific points of the game with a mind to perfect team work, base running, bunting, place hitting and every other department of the game is studied and discussed by the leading colored players which, if continued, will enable them, in the course of a few years, to cope successfully in every particular with the leading teams of the country.

The Color Line

In no other profession has the color line been drawn more rigidly than in base ball. As far back as 1872 the first colored ball player of note playing on a white team was Bud Fowler, the celebrated promoter of colored ball clubs, and the sage of base ball. Bud played on a New Castle, Pennsylvania, team that year. Later the Walker Brothers, Fleet and Weldy, played on prominent college teams of the West. Fleet Walker has the distinction of being the only known colored player that ever played in one of the big leagues. In 1884 Walker caught for Toledo in the old American Association. At this time the Walker brothers and Bud Fowler were the only negroes in the profession.

In 1886 Frank Grant joined Buffalo, of the International League.

In 1887 no less than twenty colored ball players scattered among the different smaller leagues of the country.

With Walker, Grant, Stovey, Fowler, Higgins and Renfro in the International League, White, W. Walker, N. Higgins and R. Johnson in the Ohio League, and others in the West, made 1887 a banner year for colored talent in the white leagues. But this year marked the beginning of the elimination of colored players from white clubs. All the leagues, during the Winter of 1887 and 1888, drew the color line, or had a clause inserted in their constitutions limiting the number of colored players to be employed by each club.

JAS. BOOKER
Catcher
Philadelphia Giants

This color line has been agitated by A. C. Anson, Captain of the Chicago National League team for years. As far back as 1883, Anson, with his team, landed in Toledo, O., to play an exhibition game with the American Association team. Walker, the colored catcher, was a member of the Toledos at the time. Anson at first absolutely refused to play his nine against Walker, the colored man, until he was told he could either play with Walker on this team or take his nine off the field. Anson in 1887 again refused to play the Newark Eastern League with Stovey, the colored pitcher, in the box. Were it not for this same man Anson, there would have been a colored player in the National League in 1887. John W. Ward, of the New York club, was anxious to secure Geo. Stovey and arrangements were about completed for his transfer from the Newark club, when a bawl was heard from Chicago to New York. The same Anson, with all the venom of hate which would be worthy of a Tillman or a Vardaman of the present day, made strenuous and fruitful opposition to any proposition looking to the admittance of a colored man into the National League. Just why Adrian C. Anson, manager and captain of the Chicago National League Club, was so strongly opposed to colored players on white teams cannot be explained. His repugnant feeling, shown at every opportunity, toward colored ball players, was a source of comment through every league in the country, and his opposition, with his great popularity and power in base ball circles, hastened the exclusion of the black man from the white leagues.

PHILADELPHIA GIANTS. Season, 1902.

The colored players are not only barred from playing on white clubs, but at times games are canceled for no other reason than objections being raised by a Southern ball player, who refuses to play against a colored ball club. These men from the South who object to playing are, as a rule, fine ball players, and rather than lose their services, the managers will not book a colored team.

The colored ball player suffers great inconvenience, at times, while traveling. All hotels are generally filled from the cellar to the garret when they strike a town. It is a common occurrence for them to arrive in a city late at night and walk around for several hours before getting a place to lodge.

The situation is far different to-day in this respect than it was years ago. At one time the colored teams were accommodated in some of the best hotels in the country, as the entertainment in 1887 of the Cuban Giants at the McClure House in Wheeling, W. Va., will show.

The cause of this change is no doubt due to the condition of things from a racial standpoint. With the color question upper-most in the minds of the people at the present time, such proceedings on the part of hotel-keepers may be expected and will be difficult to remedy.

It is said on good authority that one of the leading players and a manager of the National League is advocating the entrance of colored players in the National League with a view of signing "Matthews," the colored man, late of Harvard. It is not expected that he will succeed in this advocacy of such a move, but when such actions come to notice there are grounds for hoping that

The Philadelphia Giants

Base Ball and Athletic Association, Inc.

Year	Played	Won	Lost	Tied	Pct.
1902	106	81	43	2	.653
1903	130	89	37	4	.700
1904	142	95	41	6	.699
1905	158	134	21	3	.848
1906	145	108	31	6	.745

The Philadelphia Giants have held the Championship since 1904 and will be prepared to defend the title against all comers at any time.

The "Phillies" are the premier attraction among the colored teams and their presence is eagerly looked for by many thousands in all sections of the country.

They can be booked through

SCHLICHTER & STRONG,
Booking Agents
Room 46 World Building,
New York City, or

H. WALTER SCHLICHTER,
28 S. 7th St., Phila., Pa.

some day the bar will drop and some good man will be chosen from out of the colored profession that will be a credit to all, and pave the way for others to follow.

This article would not be complete did we not mention the effort of John McGraw, manager of the New York National League, to sign a colored man for his Baltimore American League team.

While Manager McGraw was in Hot Springs, Ark., preparing to enter the season of 1901, he was attracted toward Chas. Grant, second baseman of the Columbia Giants of Chicago, who was also at Hot Springs, playing on a colored team. McGraw, whose knowledge of and capacity for base ball is surpassed by none, thought he saw in Grant a ball player and a card. With the color line so rigidly enforced in the American League, McGraw was at a loss as to how he could get Grant for his Baltimore bunch. The little Napoleon of base ball with a brain for solving intricate circumstances in base ball transactions, conceived the idea of introducing Grant in the league as an Indian. Had it not been for friends of Grant being so eager to show their esteem while the Baltimores were playing in Chicago, McGraw's little scheme would have worked nicely. As it was the bouquet tendered to Grant, which was meant as a gift for the colored man, was really his undoing. McGraw was immediately notified to release Grant at once, as colored players would not be tolerated in the league. This shows what a base ball man will do to get a winner and also shows why McGraw has been called by many, the greatest of all base ball managers.

94 Sol White's Official Base Ball Guide

ROYAL GIANTS, of Brooklyn. Season, 1906.

The following open letter was sent to President McDermit, of the Tri-State (formerly Ohio) League, by Weldy Walker, a member of the Akron, O., team of 1887, which speaks for itself.

The letter was dated March 5th, 1888. The law prohibiting the employment of colored players in the league was rescinded a few weeks later.

Steubenville, O., March 5 – Mr. McDermit, President Tri-State League – Sir: I take the liberty of addressing you because noticing in The Sporting Life that the "law," permitting colored men to sign was repealed, etc., at the special meeting held at Columbus, February 22, of the above-named League of which you are the president. I ascertaining the reason of such an action I have grievances, it is a question with me whether individual loss subserves the public good in this case. This is the only question to be considered – both morally and financially – in this, as it is, or ought to be, in all cases that convinced beyond doubt that you all, as a body of men, have not been impartial and unprejudiced in your consideration of the great and important question – the success of the "National game."

The reason I say this is because you have shown partiality by making an exception with a member of the Zanesville Club, and from this one would infer that he is the only one of the three colored players – Dick Johnson, alias Dick Neale, alias Dick Noyle, as the Sporting Life correspondent from Columbus has it; Sol White, of the Wheelings, whom I must compliment by saying was one, if not the surest hitter in the Ohio League last year, and your humble servant, who was

GRANT (Home Run) JOHNSON
Captain and Short Stop, Royal Giants

unfortunate enough to join the Akron just ten days before they busted.

It is not because I was reserved and have been denied making my bread and butter with some clubs that I speak; but it is in hopes that the action taken at your last meeting will be called up for reconsideration at your next.

The law is a disgrace to the present age, and reflect very much upon the intelligence of your last meeting, and casts derision at the laws of Ohio – the voice of the people – that says all men are equal. I would suggest that your honorable body, in case that black law is not repealed, pass one making it criminal for a colored man or woman to be found in a ball ground.

There is now the same accommodation made for the colored patron of the game as the white, and the same provision and dispensation is made for the money of them both that finds its way into the coffers of the various clubs.

There should be some broader cause – such as lack of ability, behavior and intelligence – for barring a player, rather than his color. It is for these reasons and because I think ability and intelligence should be recognized first and last – at all times and by everyone – I ask the question again why was the "law permitting colored men to sign repealed, etc.?"

Yours truly,

WELDY W. WALKER

J. W. CONNOR
Owner and Manager
Royal Giants, of Brooklyn

John W. Connor

Royal Cafe
AND
Palm Garden

176 MYRTLE AVENUE
BROOKLYN, NEW YORK

Headquarters Royal Giants.

Music and Entertainment every evening.

ROBERT FOOTES
Catcher
Royal Giants, of Brooklyn

WM. S. MONROE
3rd Baseman
Royal Giants

GEO. (CHAPPIE) JOHNSON
Catcher
Royal Giants, of Brooklyn

WM. HOLLAND
Pitcher
Royal Giants, of Brooklyn

HARRY BUCKNER
Pitcher
Royal Giants, of Brooklyn

Old Timers Compared

The colored ball players of to-day are just as fast as those of years ago. They hit as well, field as well and are just as speedy on their feet as the boys of the late '80's and early '90's were when at their best. But are they as good as the old ones were when together as a team?

It is a well known fact that a base ball team composed of all star players never won a pennant. When you see a team of all star ball players, you will find individuality a very prominent feature in their style of play. Individuality is a great hindrance to team work and without team work a team stands a poor chance of beating a bunch of ball players that play the game.

There is a vast difference in the disposition of the ball player of to-day than that of the old timers. They do not take to other athletic sports as the old boys used to do when afforded the opportunity. Swimming, rowing, boxing and sprinting contests were of frequent occurrence with the boys of the early '90's, while the players of today are satisfied to attend such contests as spectators only.

As a comparison of the merits of the old ball teams with the teams of late years, the team of 1891 called the Big Gorhams, was the best of the old bunch, and the Philadelphia Giants of 1905 the best of the colored ball players since 1891. This selection is not meant to discredit the great playing of the Cuban Giants of 1894, the Chicago Unions of 1898 and '99, the Columbia Giants of 1899 and 1900, the Cuban X-Giants of

Advertisement for the tobacco business of Manuel Camps, owner of the Cuban Stars.

1901 to 1904, but individually and collectively in the opinion of the majority of fans that have followed colored base ball from its infancy the Gorhams of 1891 and the Philadelphia Giants of 1905 were the premier of their respective times. The line-up of both teams were:

Gorhams of 1891		Phila. Giants of 1905
Clarence Williams	Catcher	James Booker
Arthur Thomas	Catcher	Tom Washington
Geo. Stovey	Pitcher	Dan McClellan
Wm. Selden	Pitcher	Andrew Foster
Wm. Malone	Pitcher	Emmett Bowman
Geo. Williams	First Base	Sol White
Sol White	Second Base	Chas. Grant
Andrew Jackson	Third Base	Wm. Monroe
Frank Grant	Short Stop	Grant Johnson
Malone or Selden	Left Field	J. Preston Hill
Oscar Jackson	Centre Field	Harry Moore
Thomas or Williams	Right Field	Bowman, McClellan or Foster

A series of games between these two teams would have been worth going miles to see and would have rivaled the late world's series which was played in Chicago.

MANUEL CAMPS
Owner and Manager
Cuban Stars

The Cubans

The Cuban teams have shown a wonderful improvement in their style of play since their first visit to this country, which is no doubt due to the observation of the style and system by which the American ball teams play the game. The Cuban players gave everything that constitute good ball playing with the exception of inside work. They are wonderful fielders, strong throwers and fast runners. They lack the baseball nerve or staying qualities, which shows so prominently in the American players and many games are deliberately thrown away by the Cubans when they think the umpire has made a mistake or when one of their number is guilty of a misplay.

Bunting was an unknown art with the Cuban player until the past two or three seasons. Now, they seem to be particularly in love with the squeeze play, and they are always pleased when the occasion offers the opportunity to pull it off.

The Cubans are great for all around work. They all seem able to play any position on the diamond and play it well.

Of the many Cuban teams that have visited America, the stronger was the Cuban Stars of Santiago de Cuba. They were organized in 1905 and composed of all Cuban players. Their American manager is Manuel Camps, of Brooklyn, N. Y. This team is the only Cuban team in the National Association of Colored Base Ball Clubs of the United States and Cuba.

The leading Cuban player in the estimation of the American public is Bustamante, short-stop of the Cuban Stars, although

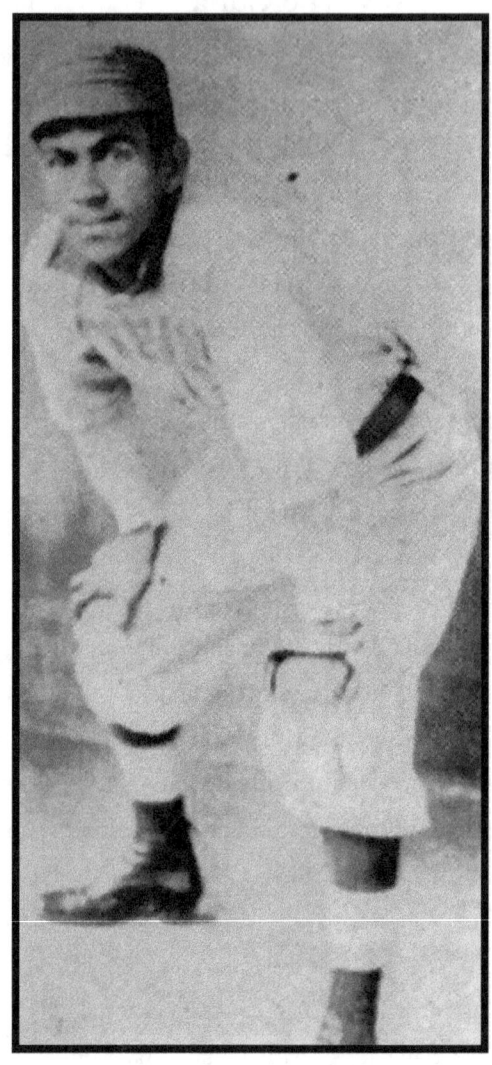

LUIS BUSTAMANTE
Short Stop
Cuban Stars

this player is not as fast as he was three seasons back. While he is still considered one of the best in the profession he does not show the form at the bat nor on bases as when he first made his appearance in America. Being a natural player his lack of form is no doubt, due to staleness.

Cuban players are in the game Winter and Summer, and of a necessity become stale in the course of a short time.

Players like Almeida, Palimino, Garcia, Valdes, Molina, Prats Perez and other stars of Cuba should take a season's rest. It would add several years to their base ball career.

PEDRO MEDINA
Catcher
Cuban Stars

How to pitch

by Andrew Foster

It has been clearly demonstrated in the history of the national game of base ball that all positions need men that can play their respective positions and play them well. But it matters not how strong the infield or outfield may be, or how fast a team is on the bases, the main strength of all base ball nines lies in their pitchers. It does seem strange that a team composed of star players of to-day are weak without some first-class pitchers. It is a common occurrence to hear or read the report of a game of ball where the headlines read, "He pitched great ball, but his support was bad," or "they never hit behind him," or "he was wild and ineffective." Sometimes the pitchers get great credit, especially when he has had support. There is always sympathy expressed for him, showing plainly the responsibility resting on his shoulders.

Any pitcher who expects to pitch regularly or play professional ball should first learn the essentials of making a pitcher.

Some people consider a young pitcher with terrific speed and a variety of curves a wonder, but the experienced base ball "fan" will watch his work for some time before they class him with the star twirlers. I have seen young pitchers at times pitch wonderful ball when receiving extraordinary support, but they never stop to think that it matters not how much speed or how fast their balls break, or how they fool the batter, that the batter is daily figuring on him and it is only a matter of time before

GEORGE (Chappie) JOHNSON
First baseman
Columbia Giants, 1899-1900

they will solve his delivery. Being used to fooling batters, some pitchers, when they get hit, become worried and they will say "they don't break right for me to-day." Everything may work wrong for awhile and people will begin to lose confidence in him, especially if he is a youngster in fast company.

So many pitchers ruin their chances by not being in condition. Condition is the main essential to pitching. Some pitchers are better in warm weather than in cold weather. A pitcher should never fully let out until his arm becomes warm and limbered up. I have lost games by not being warmed up; but what is a game, to a pitcher's arm?

This is particularly true with the young pitcher who may be called in to replace a pitcher who is being hit. Naturally every pitcher has pride, and very few object to being made a hero of. It is natural that he should want to save the game, and so is likely to forget to get into the pitching gradually and is more than likely to thus permanently injure his arm.

I have a theory of pitching that has helped me considerably. A pitcher should have control of every ball he pitches. But it matters not how good a pitcher is, he will become wild at times and can't get them over. Do not become disheartened at that, don't slacken your speed to get a ball over the plate, but teach yourself to master the weakness. Some pitchers when they have three balls and two strikes on the batter, often bring the ball straight over the plate and as the batter is always looking for it that way he will possibly "break up the game" for you. I use a curve ball mostly when in the hole. In the first place, the batter

JOHN W. PATTERSON
Manager
Columbia Giants, of Chicago, 1899-1900

is not looking for it, and secondly they will hit at a curve quicker as it may come over the plate, and if not, they are liable to be fooled. Most pitchers in the independent teams use a fast ball close to the batter which the batter can easily see will be on the in-corner of the plate and they get their eye on it very easy.

A pitcher should learn to field his position. Always try to get a ball in a position to throw it.

The real test comes when you are pitching with men on bases. Do not worry. Try to appear jolly and unconcerned. I have smiled often with the bases full with two strikes and three balls on the batter. This seems to unnerve them. In other instances, where the batter appears anxious to hit waste a little time on him, and when you think he realizes his position and everybody yelling for him to hit it out, waste a few balls and try his nerve; the majority of times you will win out by drawing him into hitting at a wide one.

I often sit on the bench and watch the opposing teams' batting practice to see how they swing at a ball and I gain a great deal by it. Try everything you can on a batter, and if he hits, don't become discouraged. Batters often have a day on and will hit any kind of ball, no matter where you put it.

The three great principles of pitching are good control, when to pitch certain balls, and where to pitch them. The longer you are in the game, the more you should gain by experience. Where inexperience will lose many games, nerve and experience will bring you out victor.

If at first you don't succeed, try again.

ANDREW FOSTER

WM. BROWN
Asst. Manager
Leland Giants, of Chicago, 1906

Art and Science of Hitting

by Grant (Home Run) Johnson

There are a number of requisites that a player should possess to be a first-class hitter, but in my opinion, two of the greatest and most essential ones are confidence and fearlessness. If, because of the reputation of the pitcher opposing you, your confidence in your ability to hit him is lacking, or you fear being hit by his wonderful speed or have the least fear in your heart at all, your success at such a time is indeed doubtful. If you possess both of these essentials, then it is an easy matter for the earnest student of hitting to acquire the science and judgment. Most young players make the natural mistake of trying to become home-run hitters and hit the ball with all the force at their command at all times with a full swing of the bat. This is a serious mistake and a great detriment to good batting.

In swinging the bat with all your might, you in a measure, lose sight of the ball and also change the course you intended the bat to go, and even if only the fraction of an inch, it will not meet the ball fairly, which results as a rule, in a comparatively easy chance for the opposing fielders. At a critical period of a game the experienced pitcher would far prefer pitching to the mighty swinger than the cool steady batter who tries to meet the ball and place it to the best advantage. My advice to young players is secure a bat which you can handle perfectly, catch well upon it and in taking your position at the plate, be sure

BERT WILLIAMS
of Williams and Walker
Manager and First baseman
W. & W. B. B. C., and all around "fan"

and stand firmly and face the pitcher, thinking you are going to hit without the least atom of fear about you. Seldom strike at the first ball pitched, as in letting it pass you get a line on the speed or curve of the pitcher. As he delivers one to your liking, try to meet it fairly, and when successful you will be surprised, and gratified, at the distance of the hit, with only ordinary force behind the swing. To improve the eye, I find bunting to be very effective, and should be practiced before each game as a player who can both hit and bunt is a very valuable man to any team.

GRANT JOHNSON

FRANK GRANT
Second baseman
for Buffalo International League team, 1888
The greatest base ball player of his age

Casey at the Bat

The outlook wasn't brilliant for the Mudville nine that day;
The score stood four to two with but one inning more to play,
And then when Cooney died at first and Barrows did the same,
A sickly silence fell upon the patrons of the game.

A straggling few got up to go in deep despair. The rest
clung to that hope which springs eternal in the human breast;
They thought if only Casey could get a whack at that –
We'd put up even money yet with Casey at the bat.

But Flynn preceded Casey, as did also Jimmie Blake,
And the former was a Lula, and latter was a cake,
So upon that stricken multitude grim melancholy sat,
For there seemed but little chance of Casey coming to the bat.

But Flynn let drive a single to the wonderment of all,
And Blake, the much despised, tore the cover off the ball;
And when the smoke was lifted, and the men saw what had occurred,
There was Johnnie safe at second and Flynn a-hugging third.

Then from five thousand throats or more there rose a lusty yell;
It rumbled through the valley, it rattled through the dell;
It knocked upon the mountain and recoiled upon the flat,
For Casey, mighty Casey, was advanc[ing] to the bat.

There was ease in Casey's manner as he stepped into his place;
There was pride in Casey's bearing and a smile on Casey's face.

W. W. WALKER
Catcher
Akron, O. League team, 1887

And when, responding to the cheers, he lightly doffed his hat,
No stranger in the crowd could doubt 'twas Casey at the bat.

Ten thousand eyes were on him as he rubbed his hands with dirt,
Five thousand tongues applauded as he wiped them on his shirt,
Then while the writhing pitcher ground the ball into his hip,
Defiance gleamed in Casey's eye, a sneer curled Casey's lip.

And now the leather-covered sphere came hurtling through the air,
And Casey stood a watching it in hauty grandeur there,
Close by the sturdy batsman the ball unheeded sped –
"That ain't my style," said Casey.
"Strike one," the umpire said.

From the benches black with people, there went up a muffled roar,
Like the beating of the storm waves on a stern and distant shore.
Kill him! Kill the umpire! shouted some one on the stand;
And its likely they'd have killed him had not Casey raised his hand.

With a smile of Christian charity great Casey's visage shone.
He stilled the rising tumult; he bade the game go on;
He signaled to the pitcher and once more the spheroid flew;
But Casey still ignored it and the umpire said, "Strike two!"

"Fraud!" cried the maddened thousands, and the echo answered fraud,
But one scornful look from Casey and the multitude was awed.

CHAMPIONSHIP CUP
International League
won by
Philadelphia Giants, season, 1906

They saw his face grow stern and cold, they saw his muscles strain,
And they knew that Casey wouldn't let that ball go by again.

The sneer has gone from Casey's lip, his teeth are clinched in hate;
He pounds with cruel violence his bat upon the plate.
And now the pitcher holds the ball and now he lets it go,
And now the air is shattered by the force of Casey's blow.

Oh! somewhere in this favored land the sun is shining bright;
The band is playing somewhere and somewhere hearts are light,
And somewhere men are laughing, and somewhere children shout,
But there is no joy in Mudville – mighty Casey has struck out.

THE ROYAL POINCIANA Base Ball Team of Palm Beach, Fla. Season, 1906. A combination hard to beat.

When Casey Slugged the Ball

Oh, you all have heard of Mudville.
    Heard of mighty Casey, too;
Of the groans amid the bleachers
    As the ball thrice past him flew;
But you haven't heard the story,
    The best story of them all,
Of the day in happy Mudville,
    When great Casey slugged the ball.

'Twas the day they played "the Giants,"
    And the score stood ten to eight;
Two men were on the bases,
    And great Casey at the plate.
"Swipe her, Casey," yelled the rooters,
    And the hero doffed his cap;
Three to win and two to tie,
    And Casey at the bat.

Mid a hush of expectation,
    Now the ball flies past his head;
Great Casey grins a sickly grin;
    "Strike one," the umpire said.
Again the pitcher raised his arm,
    Again the horse-hide flew;
Great Casey spat upon the ground,
    And the umpire said, "Strike two."

NAT C. STRONG, Secretary
National Association Colored Base Ball Clubs
of the United States and Cuba

"It's a roast," came from the grandstand,
  "He is bought without a doubt!"
"He is rotten!" roared the bleachers,
  "Throw the daylight robber out!"
"I'll break yer face," says Casey,
  "That one went below my knee;
"If I miss the next, ye blackguard
  "Ye won't live long to see."

The next one came like lightning,
  And the umpire held his breath,
For well he knew if Casey missed,
  'Twould surely mean his death!
But Casey swung to meet it,
  Backed by all his nerve and gall; –
Oh, if you had but heard the yell,
  As Casey smashed the ball!

He caught the pigskin on the nose,
  It cleared the big town lot,
It sailed above the high church tower,
  In vain the fielders sought;
And Casey didn't even run,
  He stopped awhile to talk,
And then amid the deafening cheers
  He came round in a walk.

And now he keeps a beer saloon;

132 Sol White's Official Base Ball Guide

World's Champions: Philadelphia Giants, season, 1906.

He is Mayor of the town.
The people flock to see him
　From all the country round;
And you need not look for Mudville
　On the map upon the wall,
Because the town is called Caseyville,
　Since Casey slugged the ball.

NAT WRIGHT

William Reynolds

Saloon

12th and Bainbridge Streets

PHILADELPHIA

Bell Phone Filbert 5999 D

With ten FREIHOFER bread labels, the holder is entitled to a free admission to any Freihofer base ball game.

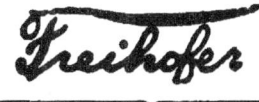

FOR A BOTTLE OF GOOD 50c. WHISKEY

Go to

McGettigan's

700 South 11th St.,

PHILADELPHIA, PA.

Golden Age whiskey a specialty

George Stæhle

Saloon

1311 Poplar St.,
PHILADELPHIA, PA.

A. A. COLEMAN
ONE OF THE "FANS"

J. W. JOHNSON

Pool Parlors
CIGARS & TOBACCO

1306 Poplar Street,
PHILADELPHIA, . . . PENNA.

BISHOP ROBINSON'S

SHAVING & HAIR CUTTING
EMPORIUM

1234 Melon St., Philadelphia, Pa.

Special Line of all kinds of Perfumery, Hair Tonic, etc., for sale at moderate prices. Razors put in order a specialty.

John J. Rouse

SALOON

700 North 13th Street
PHILADELPHIA, - PENNA.

Raymond Wilson

Cigars and Tobacco

1539½ RIDGE AVE.

BELL PHONE PHILA., PA.

Chauffeurs Rest

691 North 13th St.
OAKLEY & MARTIN, Prop.

High Grade Cigars and Tobacco
First class pool parlors

Headquarters of North Philadelphia Sports

CHOICE WINES & LIQUORS

James Bigley

13th and Ogden Streets

Fine Cigars PHILA., PA.

AMOS M. SCOTT, Prop.
H. S. SCOTT, Mgr.

Hotel Scott

Choice
Wines,
Liquors
and
Cigars

S. E. Cor. 12th & Pine Sts.

PHILADELPHIA, PA.

"Schemm's Beer"   Bell Phone

Colored Players and the League

It was clearly demonstrated that colored players possessed major league qualifications when such players as Fleet Walker, Geo. Stovey, Frank Grant and Bud Fowler as members of the International League, back in the eighties, were stars of a class "A" organization. All of these men would have been drafted by the National League or the American Association had they been of the opposite complexion. When Stovey and Walker were paired as a battery, they were considered the stars of the country. Grant and Fowler, as infielders, had no equals in the International League.

Frank Grant, in those days, was the base ball marvel. His playing was a revelation to his fellow team mates, as well as the spectators. In hitting he ranked with the best and his fielding bordered on the impossible. Grant was a born ball player. He started as a catcher when very young and it is said that during a game in Plattsburg, N. Y., while catching, he ran to a telegraph pole and climbing up about eight feet caught a foul fly. Otherwise it would have gone out of his reach over an embankment. Grant was always quiet and unassuming on the ball field, never protesting a decision of an umpire, nor resenting an action of an opposing player. He was the greatest card in the profession.

George Williams, captain of the original Cuban Giants, was a great player and would have been one of the chosen number for a big league berth. Billy Whyte, Arthur Thomas, Clarence

Williams, Ben Boyd and Ben Holmes, the crack third-baseman, would have been slated for the National League and made good.

Selden, of the Cuban Giants, of 1887, was one of the leading colored pitchers as late as 1899.

Of the players of to-day, with the same prospects for a future as the white players there would be a score or more colored ball players cavorting around the National League or American League diamonds at the present time.

As it is, the field for the colored professional is limited to a very narrow scope in the base ball world. When he looks into the future he sees no place for him on the Chicago Americans or Nationals (champions), nor the Athletics (American), or New York (National, ex-champions), even were he superior to Lajoie, or Wagner, Waddell or Mathewson, Kling or Schrock. Consequently, he loses interest. He knows that, so far shall I go, and no farther, and, as it is with the profession, so it is with his ability.

In naming a few of the many colored players of Major League calibre, we are not unmindful of those who are yet to come and are held back because of the small number of colored teams.

Of the catchers at present, the veteran, Clarence Williams, is very good, owing to his many years of base ball he would be taken as a good man for young pitchers: George (Chappie) Johnson, Bob Footes; Robinson, of Leland Giants, Petway, of Philadelphia Giants.

There are many colored pitchers who would no doubt land in the big league. McClellan, Bowman, Foster, Holland, Merritt, George Washington (Georgia Rabbit), Ball, Wilson, Davis and

Buckner; the colored profession has great all-round players in Monroe, Bowman, Wright, Smith, Moore, G. Johnson, Talbert, P. Hill, C. Grant, Harris, Nelson, Francis, Patterson, Earle and many others.

Notes
Who's Who in the Sol White Guide

Page 8: "S. K. GOVERN" A native of St. Croix in the Danish West Indies, Stanislaus Kostka Govern (1854-1924) came to the United States as a teenager and enjoyed varied careers as a head waiter, actor, journalist, and baseball manager. He was heavily involved in black baseball for at least a decade, working with the Manhattan Base Ball Club of Washington, one of the Cuban Giants' predecessor clubs, from 1881 to 1884, the Cuban Giants themselves from 1885 to 1889, the National Colored League (as a director) in 1887, and the Big Gorhams in 1891. See Rory Costello, "S. K. Govern," SABR Baseball Biography Project. (http://sabr.org/bioproj/person/af52b171)

Page 12: "BEN HOLMES" Benjamin F. Holmes was born in King and Queen County, Virginia, in 1858, and began his baseball career with the Douglas club of Wahington, D. C., in 1875. By 1883 he was playing third base for the Washington Manhattans, another of the Cuban Giants' predecessor teams. "A fair batsman and good base runner," in 1885 he became the Cuban Giants' first captain, and continued to play for them through 1890 ("Good Game Promised by the Reorganized Cuban Giants," *Trenton Evening Times*, May 9, 1886, 8). At the age of 88 he was a guest of honor at the 1946 Black World Series, and furnished a baseball used in the 1888 black championship series to be thrown out by Joe Louis as the ceremonial first pitch ("Doby Hits Homer In Second Game; Eagles Win 7-4," *Norfolk Journal and Guide*, September 28, 1946, 12).

Page 14: "GEORGE WILLIAMS" George L. Williams (1864-1918) played for the Washington Manhattans and Philadelphia Orions before joining the Cuban Giants in 1885. The following year he became their captain. Before the 1887 season he was approached by both the Minneapolis Millers of the Northwestern League and the Oswego Starchboxes of the International League, but turned them down to remain with the Cuban Giants through the 1889 season ("Base Ball Gossip," *Trenton Evening Times*, February 1, 1887, 1). Like many of his teammates he moved to the York

Monarchs of the Eastern Interstate League in 1890, winning the batting title with a .386 average. He spent 1891 with the Big Gorhams, then in 1892 joined the Philadelphia police department, becoming its first black detective in 1909. In 1918 he was shot and killed in the line of duty ("Detective Slain Battling Thugs—George L. Williams, Former Cuban Giants Baseball Player, Is Shot," *Philadelphia Inquirer*, January 10, 1918, 6).

Page 16: "WILLIAM WHYTE" William T. Whyte (1860-1936) served as pitcher and outfielder for the St. Louis Black Stockings and Boston Resolutes before joining the Cuban Giants in 1885. He stayed with them through 1893 (spending 1890 with the York Monarchs, where he went 11-5 with a 3.02 ERA in the Eastern Interstate League), and retired to Trenton, New Jersey, after that.

Page 18: "CLARENCE WILLIAMS" One of the most important figures in early black baseball, Clarence Williams (1866-1934) played professional baseball from 1882 until 1913, from age 16 to age 47. In between he played for the Cuban Giants, York Monarchs, Big Gorhams, Cuban X-Giants, Philadelphia Giants, and Paterson Smart Set, and took several winter trips to Cuba. In his youth was regarded as "a heavy batsman, fine base runner and good catcher" ("Good Game Promised," op. cit.). He was very popular, known both for his comedy coaching and for his quick temper. Even in his mid-forties, at the end of his career, Clarence Williams was still considered "a strong and heady baseball player, in the game every minute, and despite his weight and age, is still able to give a strong account of himself in a game" ("Clarence Williams' Clan Too Fast for the Locals," *Middletown Daily Times-Press*, June 29, 1912, 8).

Page 20: "GEORGE PARAGO" Born in Charlottesville, Virginia, in 1861, George A. Parago first played professionally as a first baseman and catcher for the Keystone Athletic club of Philadelphia, then became a pitcher/outfielder for the Cuban Giants, where he stayed through the 1888 season. He was praised for "making some very difficult catches" in the outfield "with great style and ease" ("Good Game Promised," op. cit.).

Page 22: "ARTHUR THOMAS (Deceased)" A very tall player (6'4", according to Sol White), Arthur Thomas (1864-1895) first caught for the Manhattan Base Ball Club of Washington, D. C., at the age of 15 in 1880. He joined the West End club of Long Branch, New Jersey, in 1881 and 1882, and in 1883 rejoined the Manhattans under S. K. Govern before moving with Govern to the Cuban Giants in 1885. With the York Monarchs in 1890, Thomas hit .333 and led the league with 26 doubles and 11 triples, and finished second in slugging percentage with .567. After leaving big-time baseball Thomas settled in Trenton, New Jersey, where he caught for and captained both black and white semipro teams. He died in Trenton of consumption (tuberculosis) at the age of 30 on August 8, 1895 ("Died," *Trenton Evening Times*, August 11, 1895, 5; "Observations from the Grandstand," *Trenton Evening Times*, August 9, 1896, 3).

Page 24: "WILLIAM MALONE" William H. Malone (1867-1917) first played professionally for the Philadelphia Pythians of the National Colored League in 1887 before joining the Cuban Giants in 1888 and 1889, the York Monarchs in 1890, the Big Gorhams in 1891, and the Page Fence Giants in 1895.

Page 26: "BENJ. BOYD" A veteran of the original Cuban Giants, Benjamin F. Boyd was born in Maryland in 1858, and started his baseball career in Washington, D. C., in 1874. "A good general player" and versatile infielder, he joined S. K. Govern's Manhattan Base Ball Club in 1883, and played for the Cuban Giants (1885-1889), the York Monarchs (1890), and Big Gorhams (1891).

Page 28: "JOHN FRYE (Deceased)" When he appeared briefly for the Reading Actives of the Interstate Association late in the 1883 season, John H. Frye (1864-1904) became the fifth known African American to play in organized baseball in the United States. He spent most of his career with the Cuban Giants, including a stint of three straight years in organized baseball from 1889 to 1891. He also played for white teams, including Lewiston of the 1886 Pennsylvania State Association. Frye retired from baseball after the 1896 season and moved to Culpeper County, Virginia, where he died on June 10, 1904 ("Bits for the Fans," *Harrisburg Telegraph*, June 11, 1904, 8).

Page 30: "HARRY JOHNSON" Born in 1860, he played semipro ball in Washington, D. C., before coming to the Cuban Giants. He was described as "a second Dunlap, covering more ground than ever was seen by any colored 2d baseman on the road, fair batsman, good base runner, and expert thrower" ("Good Game Promised," op. cit.). He played for the Cuban Giants from 1886 through 1890.

Page 32: "JOHN M. BRIGHT" A co-owner of the Cuban Giants beginning in 1886, John M. Bright (1856-1913) took over sole ownership upon the death of Walter I. Cook in 1888. Sol White had a mixed opinion of Bright. In 1929 he wrote that he would "class Bright as the leading spirit of his day in keeping the game before the public," but also called him "extremely selfish" and a sharp dealer ("The Grand Old Game," *New York Amsterdam News*, December 18, 1929, 17).

Page 34: "POP WATKINS" John McCreary "Pop" Watkins (1870?–1924) was a legendary figure in early black baseball circles. His playing career petered out after he suffered a broken leg in a game in Oil City, Pennsylvania, in 1907. Watkins became known for two things: his comedic coaching, and his training of young players. For many years he ran a team called the Havana Red Sox, which played mostly in upstate New York, and served as the proving grounds for a number of future Negro league stars. See "'Pop' Watkins Is World's Greatest Base Ball Scout," *Baltimore Afro-American*, July 13, 1923, 15, and "'Pop' Watkins Dies in South," *Watertown Daily Times*, February 26, 1924, 18.

Page 36: "J. GARCIA (Deceased)" White originally identified this player as "A. Garcia," but his name was in fact John Garcia. He was a Cuban immigrant and quite possibly the only genuine Cuban ever to play for the Cuban Giants. On October 1, 1904, during a Cuban Giants game against a team called the Woodhulls at Kings Park in Jamaica, Long Island, caught a foul ball, then collapsed. His teammates immediately carried him across the street to St. Mary's Hospital, but he was pronounced dead on arrival, apparently of heart failure. His death was front page news in the *New York Times*. Within a few days it emerged that he had had two wives, one black and one white. They unaware of each other's existence until both tried to claim his body ("Caught the Ball and Died," *New York Times*, October 2, 1904, 1; "Two Claimants for Body," *Brooklyn Daily Eagle*, October 7, 1904, 19).

Page 39: "CHASE LYONS" He pitched from 1899 to 1905, mostly for Chicago teams.

Page 41: "CUBAN X-GIANTS Season, 1905" The image from the original edition has been replaced by a (much clearer) postcard version of the same photograph. Standing L to R: Dangerfield Talbert, Ray Wilson, Edward B. Lamar, Robert Jordan, John Patterson, Clarence Williams; Kneeling L to R: Frank Grant, Bobby Winston, Johnny Hill, John Nelson, Harry Buckner.

Page 44: "E. B. LAMAR, Jr." Floyd J. Calvin, presumably getting his information from Sol White, called Edward B. Lamar "not a sportsman, but merely a follower. His job was principally that of bookkeeping." His brother was the catcher Pete Lamer (the two brothers seem to have spelled their names differently), who enjoyed a couple of very brief cups of coffee with the Chicago Cubs, and also played a number of years in the minors and on the semipro circuit ("Ed Hughes' Column," *Brooklyn Daily Eagle*, January 13, 1935, D2). E. B. Lamar was one of the most important baseball ambassadors between the United States and Cuba. He was the first to organize regular trips to Cuba by black teams, beginning in 1900 and continuing into the 1920s. He also booked and managed several traveling Cuban teams in the U.S. Sol White later wrote that Lamar "was held in the highest regard by the players ("The Grand Old Game," op. cit.).

Page 46: "RAY WILSON" Ray Wilson and Sol White knew each other well. They were teammates with the Cuban X-Giants, and Wilson played for White's Philadelphia Giants in 1907 and 1908. White would later describe Wilson as "tall and well built, standing about six-two in his sox [sic]. In playing first base he was graceful, was good on ground balls and had a reach the fans used to talk about, and are still talking about" ("Old-Time Baseball Players, *New York Amsterdam News*, March 6, 1929, 6). He captained the Cuban X-Giants for several years, and in 1909 succeeded White as captain and manager of the Philadelphia Giants.

Page 48: "JOHN NELSON" Though he is fairly obscure even among historians, John Nelson performed at the top level of black professional baseball for two decades, from his start with the New York Gorhams in 1887 to his last appearance for the Genuine Cuban Giants in 1908. Nelson and Sol White are the only two players known to have appeared in both the National Colored League of 1887 and the National Association of Colored Baseball Clubs of 1907 and 1908.

Page 50: "JOHN HILL" A light-hitting glove man, Hill played from 1900 to 1910 for a number of east coast teams. Best known as a third baseman for the Cuban X-Giants, he accompanied them on two trips to Cuba. He was killed during a fight with a companion in Philadelphia in 1922 (Untitled item, *Chicago Defender*, October 7, 1922, 10).

Page 52: "W. S. PETERS" The original first baseman of the Chicago Unions, William S. Peters (1867-1933) also served as their manager from 1890 to 1900. Frank Leland took over the club in 1901 and changed its name to Union Giants; three years later Peters started his own Union Giants club, sparking a legal battle between Leland and Peters that resulted in Leland renaming his team the Leland Giants. Peters ran his Union Giants, mostly as a traveling team in the Midwest, until he was struck by a car and killed in 1933 (*Frank Leland's Chicago Giants Base Ball Club*, op. cit., 2-4; "Fight for the Union Giants, *Chicago Daily Tribune*, June 7, 1904, 8; "Peters, Baseball Man, in Fatal Accident," *Chicago Defender*, April 8, 1933, 3).

Page 54: "HARRY HYDE" Harry Hyde played for the Chicago Unions and Union Giants from 1896 to 1906, then in a couple of games for the St. Paul Gophers in 1907.

Page 56: "DAVID WYATT" Dave Wyatt (1874-1950) played and managed in the 1890s and 1900s, but he made his greatest impact in journalism. Though his work for a range of African American newspapers in the first two decades of the 20th century was never collected into a book, he was probably Sol White's closest rival as a writer and authority on early black baseball. Wyatt was also closely involved in the 1901 attempt to smuggle Charlie Grant into the American League as a Native American (see page 93).

Page 60: "ROBERT JACKSON" Robert Jackson caught for the Chicago Unions from 1896 to 1900.

Page 68: "PHILADELPHIA GIANTS. Champions. Season, 1905." Standing L to R: Harry Smith, Harry Moore, Emmett Bowman, Sol White, Tom Washington, Danny McClellan; Seated middle L to R: Grant Johnson, Charlie Grant, H. Walter Schlichter, Rube Foster, Pete Hill; Seated front Bill Monroe, James Booker.

Page 72: "H. WALTER SCHLICHTER" A sportswriter for the *Philadelphia Item* (see ad on page 62), Henry Walter Schlichter (1866-1944) was a boxing promoter and co-founder of the Philadelphia Giants with Sol White and Harry Smith. In 1909, after a disagreement with White, Shclichter took over sole control of the team, and White was blacklisted by the National Association. They eventually reconciled and kept up a correspondence for many years. White would later write warmly about Schlichter, praising him as "my ideal of an owner of a colored baseball team" (Sol White, "The Grand Old Game," *New York Amsterdam News*, December 18, 1929, 17).

Page 74: "CHAS. Kid CARTER" He pitched from 1900 to 1906 for east coast teams, including the Cuban X-Giants, Philadelphia Giants, and Brooklyn Royal Giants.

Page 76: "ANDREW (Rube) FOSTER" A colossal figure in African American baseball history, Rube Foster (1879-1930) was the most celebrated black pitcher at the time White was putting his *Guide* together.

Foster would go on to found one of the great black baseball dynasties, the Chicago American Giants, and in 1920 he organized the first truly national Negro league. In 1981 he was elected to the National Baseball Hall of Fame.

Page 78: "CHARLES GRANT" Most famous as the player John McGraw tried to sneak into the major leagues as a Native American (see page 93), Grant was a fine defensive second baseman but only a fair hitter. Sol White would later remember him as an especially sure-handed fielder. "I will give any 'fan' a good ten-cent cigar," he wrote, "who will call my attention or, rather, recall my memory to an error on a ground ball or a muffed fly by Charley Grant" ("Old-Time Baseball Players," *New York Amsterdam News*, March 6, 1929, 8).

Page 80: "J. P. HILL" A mainstay of three of the greatest blackball teams (Sol White's Philadelphia Giants of 1904-1907, the Chicago Leland Giants of 1908-1910, and the Chicago American Giants of 1911-1918), John Preston Hill (1882-1951) was a celebrated slugger and outfielder. He previewed the coming lively ball era with the Detroit Stars in 1919, knocking 28 home runs over a cozy right field fence in just 80 games, with 16 of them coming in 38 games against top black teams. He was also an accomplished manager. In 2006 he was elected to the National Baseball Hall of Fame.

Page 82: "DAN McCLELLAN" This lefthander pitched in fast company from 1903 to 1913, spending his best years with the Philadelphia Giants. In the 1920s he managed another team called the Philadelphia Giants (with no connection to the great team of 1902-1911), which actually played most of its games in New England.

Page 84: "EMMETT BOWMAN" A truly versatile utility player who pitched and played eight positions for the Cuban X-Giants, Philadelphia Giants, and Brooklyn Royal Giants from 1905 through 1911. Sol White said of him in 1912: "I have put him in the box one day and placed him behind the bat the next against the strongest teams, and he showed up equally strong in both departments. At any position on the infield he was sensational, and there was no better outfielder in the country." Bowman died of tuberculosis in 1912 at the age of 26 ("Ballplayer Bowman Dead," *New York Age*, March 7, 1912, 6; Wyatt, "Death in the Game," op. cit.).

Page 88: "JAS. BOOKER" James "Pete" Booker (1886-1922) was a catcher and first baseman for several top teams from 1905 to 1917.

Page 90: "PHILADELPHIA GIANTS. Season, 1902." Back L to R; Farrell (first name unknown), John Nelson, Sol White, Kid Carter, William Warrick. Middle L to R: W. Smith, Frank Grant, H. Walter Schlichter, William Bell, Harry Smith, Andrew Payne. Front L to R: Day (first name unknown), Pete Burns.

Page 96: "GRANT (Home Run) JOHNSON" Grant U. Johnson (1872-1963) was the best everyday player in black baseball from 1895 to 1909, and perhaps the first great black ballplayer who never played in a white league. In 1894 he became "Home Run Johnson" by clouting 60 round-trippers for the independent (and racially mixed) Findlay Sluggers. In 1895 he and Bud Fowler, the team's two black players, moved to Adrian, Michigan, to found the Page Fence Giants—and Johnson would spend the rest of his career in the blackball world. For the next 15 years, if you wanted to build a championship-caliber African American ball club, you pretty much had to get Johnson, or it wasn't going to work. His lengthy resumé of success includes the 1899 Chicago Columbia Giants; the 1903 Cuban X-Giants, recognized colored champions; the legendary Philadelphia Giants of 1905; the champion Brooklyn Royal Giants of 1908 and 1909; the 1910 Leland Giants; and the great Lincoln Giants of 1913—not to mention the pennant-winning Habana clubs of the 1908/09 and 1911/12 Cuban League, which Johnson captained.

Page 98: "JOHN W. CONNOR" John Wilson Connor (1875-1926) owned the Royal Café, a private club and cabaret (see ad on page 98). In 1903 he took over the Niantic Base Ball Club in Brooklyn Heights; in 1904 he renamed them the Royal Giants, presumably to tie in with his other business. After the 1912 season he sold his interest in the Royals to Nat C. Strong, who had cornered the eastern independent baseball market ("Connor Retires from Baseball," *New York Age*, March 13, 1913, 6). But in 1919 he came back to baseball with a bang, teaming up with fellow magnate Barron D. Wilkins to finance a reorganization of the Atlantic City Bacharach Giants that made them into a powerhouse ("Saloonmen Become Baseball Promoters," *New York Age*, April 26, 1919, 1).

Page 100: "ROBERT FOOTES" A catcher for the Chicago Unions and Union Giants from 1895 to 1903, Footes moved to the east coast for the last part of his career, playing for the Philadelphia Giants and Brooklyn Royal Giants from 1903 to 1909.

Page 101: "WM. S. MONROE" An on-field comedian, inveterate trash-talker, and (incidentally) brilliant infielder at three positions, Bill Monroe (1878-1915) was always the focal point of attention on any team he joined. As Sol White later wrote, Monroe "was a natural comedian. He would pull some of the funniest stunts on the ball field you ever witnessed. He had a voice like a fog-horn, which could be heard blocks from the ball park. When not doing funny business, he would be having verbal spats with the bleachers or umpire" ("Our Baseball Leagues," *New York Amsterdam News*, February 20, 1929, 6).

Page 102: "GEO. (CHAPPIE) JOHNSON" George Johnson, Jr. (1877-1949), commonly known as "Chappie" or "Rat," hailed from Bellaire, Ohio, the same hometown as Sol White. He was a defensive specialist and an early adopter of shin guards. Johnson caught at the highest levels of black baseball from 1896 to 1915, and organized barnstorming teams for many years after that.

Page 103: "WM. HOLLAND" A lefthanded pitcher from 1894 to 1896 for the Chicago Unions, Page Fence Giants, Algona Brownies, and Brooklyn Royal Giants.

Page 104: "HARRY BUCKNER" Harry E. Buckner (1872-1938) was an outfielder/pitcher from 1896 to 1918, a heavy hitter who played several winters in Cuba. His brother William "Doc" Buckner was the trainer for the Chicago White Sox for many years, and Harry would go into the same line of work, training the Milwaukee Brewers of the American Association in the 1930s.

Page 106: "Le Flor de Manuel Camps" This is an advertisement for the tobacco business of Manuel Camps, owner of the Cuban Stars (see page 107).

Page 108: "MANUEL CAMPS" A Cuban immigrant and cigar manufacturer, Manuel Camps (1868-1943) collaborated with E. B. Lamar to found the Cuban Stars of Santiago de Cuba in 1906. In doing so he signed Cuban players away from Abel Linares and helped signal the death knell of the All-Cubans teams that Linares had been bringing to the U.S. for several years. Camps retained ownership of the Cuban Stars teams through 1909, and also served as an officer of the National Association of Colored Base Ball Clubs of the United States and Cuba.

Page 110: "LUIS BUSTAMANTE" One of the more celebrated Cuban players of the 1900s, Bustamante was a cannon-armed, slick-fielding shortstop who played from 1901 to 1912 in the Cuban League and 1904 to 1913 in the United States. The *Harrisburg Patriot* opined in 1906 that "Bustamante, the little shortstop of the Cuban nine, is one of the best players seen in the position in this city for a long time and if he does not get into faster company it will be because of race prejudice" ("Chat About the Tri-State Players," op. cit.). He was part of the inaugural class inducted into the Cuban baseball hall of fame in 1939.

Page 112: "PEDRO MEDINA" Medina was actually a pitcher. He went 7-8 over three seasons in the Cuban League and 2-5 in blackball competition for the Cuban Stars in 1906-07.

Page 116: "JOHN W. PATTERSON" In a professional career that lasted from 1890 to 1908, John Patterson (1872-1940) played for the Page Fence Giants, the Columbia Giants of Chicago (which he also managed), the Chicago Union Giants, Philadelphia Giants, and Cuban X-Giants, and also played in Cuba. James H. Smith, a former teammate, called Patterson a "good hitter and excellent base runner," and "one of the brainiest and shrewdest leaders of any team of color" ("The Past and Present in Baseball," *Indianapolis Freeman*, May 28, 1910, 7). He retired to Battle Creek, Michigan, where he coached the Battle Creek High School baseball team to the state championship, then became a policeman in the Battle Creek Police Department. Patterson died in 1940 as a result of injuries suffered while trying to capture an escaped mental patient (" 'Pat' Patterson Is Dead," *Chicago Defender*, September 7, 1940, 20).

Page 118: "WM. BROWN" The traveling manager of the Chicago Union Giants and Leland Giants from 1902 to 1906, praised by James H. Smith for his geniality and "good leadership" ("The Past and Present in Baseball," op. cit.). Dave Wyatt called Brown "the best handler of ball players that I have seen yet. He was a strict disciplinarian and commanded the respect of all players, and his knowledge of the traits of different individuals went a long ways towards solving knotty problems" (David Wyatt, "Sparks from the Diamond," *Indianapolis Freeman*, January 22, 1910, 7).

Page 120: "BERT WILLIAMS" A vaudeville performer, singer, and comedian, Bert Williams (1874-1922) became famous as half of the celebrated "Williams & Walker" duo. Like later entertainers such as Louis Armstrong and Bill "Bojangles" Robinson, Williams was a fan and patron of black baseball. In 1909 he was scheduled to umpire a benefit game that Sol White was helping to organize on behalf of Bud Fowler, who was suffering from a serious illness (Lester A. Walton, "In the Sporting World," *New York Age*, March 25, 1909, 6).

Page 122: "FRANK GRANT" Probably the greatest everyday black ballplayer before Home Run Johnson, Ulysses Franklin Grant (1865-1937) played six consecutive years in organized baseball, a record for an avowedly black player that would last for six decades. Despite a smallish frame (at 5'7", 155 pounds, "he was not of the strong rugged type," as Sol White would later write) Grant was a fine hitter with some power, compiling a career minor league average of .336 and a slugging percentage of .487. He was inducted into the National Baseball Hall of Fame in 2006.

Page 124: "W. W. WALKER" Probably best-known as the brother of Moses Fleetwood Walker, Weldy Wilberforce Walker (1860-1937), like Fleet, played college baseball for Oberlin and Michigan and briefly appeared for the Toledo Blue Stockings of the American Association, a major league, in 1884. He played for a couple of minor league teams, and penned an open letter to the president of the Ohio State League (reproduced by White on page 94) protesting against the color line that had been newly drawn in that circuit. The Walker brothers later became exponents of the "Back-to-Africa" movement, and together published the book *Our Home Colony: A Treatise on the Past, Present, and Future of the Negro Race in America* (1908).

Page 128: "THE ROYAL POINCIANA Base Ball Team of Palm Beach, Fla. Season, 1906." Standing L to R: Charlie Grant, Emmett Bowman; Kneeling L to R: Unknown, Sol White, Chappie Johnson, unknown, Bill Monroe, Rube Foster; Sitting L to R: Danny McClellan, unknown, unknown, Pete Hill. Beginning in the 1900s, two luxury resorts in Palm Beach, Florida, the Breakers Hotel and the Royal Poinciana Hotel, staged a series between rival black baseball teams every winter, usually from late January to March. They hired many of the top African American professionals in the country, sometimes importing whole teams from the north. The "Cocoanut League," as it was known, lasted well into the 1920s.

Page 130: "NAT C. STRONG" The dominant independent baseball promoter on the east coast for thirty years, Nat C. Strong (1874-1935) controlled booking for many semipro venues and clubs as well as African American teams. In later years Sol White, who had ran afoul of Strong in 1909 when he managed an "outlaw" team, the Quaker Giants, would have some choice words about Strong: "For several years this mirage of colored baseball has lured owners of teams to streams of disaster and has stood by and laughed at their discomfiture. There is not a man in the country who has made as much money from colored ball-playing as Nat Strong, and yet he is the least interested in its welfare" ("Our Baseball Leagues," *New York Amsterdam News*, January 23, 1929, 7).

Page 132: "WORLD'S CHAMPIONS; PHILADELPHIA GIANTS. SEASON, 1906." Standing L to R: William Binga, Ed Wilson?, Sol White, Rube Foster, Nate Harris. Kneeling L to R: Danny McClellan, Pete Hill, Pete Booker, Harry Moore, Emmett Bowman, Robert Jordan. The "World's Champion" jerseys seem to have been inspired by the failure of the World Series-winning New York Giants to answer Schlichter's challenge (see page 59).

Page 135: "...ten Freihofer bread labels..." Advertisement for the business owned by William Freihofer, president of the International League of Independent Professional Base Ball Clubs of 1906 and owner of the Philadelphia Professionals white semipro club; Freihofer Bakeries still exists today.

Page 136: "A. A. COLEMAN" It's unclear what business Coleman, "one of the fans," was advertising here. He was involved in baseball, and not just as a fan: in 1908 he organized a Philadelphia club called the Quaker Giants (not be confused with the 1906 club owned by the McMahons), which Sol White managed in 1909 ("They Are Now the Quaker Giants," *Philadelphia Inquirer*, March 31, 1908, 10).

www.ingramcontent.com/pod-product-compliance
Lightning Source LLC
Chambersburg PA
CBHW071202070526
44584CB00019B/2887